JANCIS ROBINSON'S
FOOD AND WINE ADVENTURES

Books by Jancis Robinson
The Wine Book
The Great Wine Book
Masterglass
Vines, Grapes and Wines

JANCIS ROBINSON'S
FOOD AND WINE ADVENTURES

Illustrated by
John Lawrence

HEADLINE

For my parents,
who made me think the pheasant, salmon and raspberries
of Cumberland were commonplace.

First published in Great Britain in 1987
by HEADLINE BOOK PUBLISHING PLC

Robinson, Jancis
    Food and wine adventures.
    1. Food   2. Beverages
    I. Title
    641   TX353

    ISBN 0-7472-0030-0

                HEADLINE BOOK PUBLISHING PLC
                        Headline House
                  79 Great Titchfield Street
                      London W1P 7FN

            Typeset by Rapidset & Design Ltd., London
         Printed & Bound By Lee Fung Asco, Hong Kong

CONTENTS

INTRODUCTION

'Wine is one of the most civilized things in the world, and one of the material things of the world that has been brought to the greatest perfection, and which offers a greater range of enjoyment and appreciation than, possibly, any other purely sensory thing that may be purchased.' ERNEST HEMINGWAY

I love food and adore wine and believe very strongly that, in this country at least, the gulf between these symbiotic subjects is far too wide. This book, written by a true enthusiast, is an attempt to narrow that gap in a way that is useful to anyone who cares about what they eat and drink.

Those of us who decided long ago that wine is not only the drink capable of giving the most sensuous and intellectual pleasure, but also the one that goes best with food, inhabit exciting but unexplored territory. Although most of us are lucky enough to eat several times a day, and many of us enjoy wine almost every day too, we receive surprisingly little training in how to get the most out of the business of tasting, consuming and — the thrust of this book — matching the component parts of a meal.

There is genuine excitement, adventure and pleasure to be had, not only from getting the most out of each component, but in registering how they interact so as to get most pleasure out of the combination, whether they're complementary or contrasting. This is no dry-as-dust analysis though, but more of a sumptuous, hedonistic exercise of the senses, the brain and the soul.

I have long thought that the way we live now does little to develop our use or understanding of the closely related senses of taste and smell. These under-used senses are capable of giving much pleasure, several times a day, yet the great majority of the population have no idea how to use them. Two of my previous offerings, *The Wine Book* and *Masterglass*, have tried to do something towards correcting this sad state of affairs.

This book is much more personal — a collection of widely differing experiences I've had, most of them successful, others less so, in analysing the marriage of different wines with different foods. It is organized chronologically from breakfast to supper, and covers everything from sausages to smoked salmon. Its aim — apart from, I hope, providing a good read — is to outline some ground rules and to suggest some points of departure for experimentation. The few rules that exist in common currency concerning how wine is served with food could do with some brushing up. My own experiences of 'white wine with fish and red wine with meat' are related in Chapters 9 and 19. And I have long been an adversary of the 'rule' that all whites should be served well chilled and all reds *chambré*. The weight of a wine (and there are some wines that are just *too* heavy for most foods) seems to me a much more important factor than its colour in determining both its ideal serving temperature and the sort of food it best accompanies.

This is not to say that I'm a determined iconoclast at the table. In my experience most famous combinations of food and wine work extremely well, even if some of them — Yquem and Roquefort, for instance — sound bizarre at first; they have been tested by generations of gastronomes, after all. But there are many other even less obvious and, in some cases, more useful combinations which work just as well. Many humbler sweet wines, for instance, can transform a sector of good Cheddar into a sophisticated cheese and a sweet course combined.

Wherever possible, I have tried to give sound scientific reasons for successful (and unsuccessful) combinations of food and wine, so that a single idea can be adapted and elaborated upon. It is in the nature of such a sensual form of enjoyment that its pleasures are limitless.

One last thing. Although wine is my favourite drink, I nominate water as my close second. Whatever wine I drink at the table, I tend to drink at least as much water. This stops me doing anything as foolish as quenching my thirst with a heavily taxed liquid that does the brain cells and liver no good at all if consumed with *too* much enthusiasm.

Santé.

CHAPTER ONE

THE PERFECT BREAKFAST
KIPPERS & KRUG

*'Taking well known brands all round, I do not know that I
was more faithful to any than to Krug. I began my fancy
for it with a [18] '65, which memory represents as
being, though dry, that "winy wine" as Thackeray
describes it, which champagne ought to be, but too seldom
is.'* GEORGE SAINTSBURY, NOTES ON A CELLAR BOOK

Some combinations of food and wine taste as though they're
made in heaven. Others sound as though they're made in hell
but, if consumed in the right circumstances, can taste divine.

I remember the first day back in western Europe after two
weeks' camping in the Soviet Union, which had themselves
been preceded by two or three weeks' working our way east-
ward fuelled by ever poorer cuisines. The Soviet diet was so
restricted that I can remember sitting under windswept
canvas outside Leningrad chewing sour black bread and surprisingly good plum jam dreaming about, of all things, a
bowl of porridge. Small wonder then that on that first day
'out' in Finland we ate six meals, all of them at very simple
local equivalents of motorway service stations. We washed
down the last of them with some extremely modest, not to
say dubious, Beaujolais, but nothing could have tasted more
delicious than that open prawn sandwich and the cheap
blended *p'tit rouge.*

I was to enjoy another unconventional but wonderfully
sybaritic combination of fish and wine many years later,
thanks to John Arlott, that great old man of cricket and wine
(he repudiates wine expertise far more than he need). His
wine merchant friend Christopher Fielden cottoned on
sooner than most to the fact that I might be around the wine
business long enough to be worth cultivating. In the heat of
the 1976 summer he accordingly invited myself and a fellow
wine merchant, Richard Taylor, to inspect one of his then
suppliers, Chantovent in Bonnières-sur-Seine outside Paris.
We were to travel by overnight ferry both ways via South-
ampton on a route whose geographical *raison d'être* seems, in
retrospect, a mite unclear, but whose social justification — a
stopover *chez* Arlott there and back — was delightfully com-
prehensible. We sped along dusty Hampshire lanes, scatter-
ing pheasant drowsily enjoying the lengthening rays of an
orb already signposting our immediate destination, The Old
Sun.

Before his isolation — a retreat on Alderney — John Arlott lived in an old coaching inn in Alresford, set round three sides of a yard where one could almost hear clips, clops and horsy snorts still. The house was full of fascinating evidence of John's wide range of, mainly artistic, interests.

It was assumed I would be most interested in one particular section of the house, however — the cellar. The proportions of these interlocking chambers were just as they had been originally, when the house was a busy inn, the low ceilings being more suited to squat sixteenth-century innkeepers than to a twentieth-century figure of Arlott grandeur. The mind-boggling vast collection of bottles was reached via a flight of wooden steps so precipitous that I could well understand why John thought it prudent to bring up a whole evening's bottles at a time. We rose from our subterranean foray clinking several (I think it was six) bottles of the Arlott favourite, Beaujolais.

There my memory starts to fade, which is perhaps not surprising. I do remember Monsieur Arlott telling me that his dream was to be driven round the hills of Beaujolais by a beautiful French *chauffeuse* in long leather gloves. Or did I imagine the gloves?

What I remember most clearly however is the return journey. A horrid overnight boat trip from Le Havre left me feeling uncomfortably travelworn and in need of a something as refreshing as a cool shower, which is just what I got. The Arlott household had given breakfast to recent Channel-crossers before. Waiting for us was a bottle of Krug, the old sort of Krug, sitting stodgily and dependably in a conventional champagne bottle labelled Private Cuvée. John Arlott had just finished his monograph, *Krug — House of Champagne*, and we were, I suspect, drinking some of his reward.

The wine was glorious. I am a great Krugophile anyway, and persisted with Private Cuvée's rather flashier successor, Grande Cuvée, until it had mellowed into a suitably grand state of maturity after its launch a year or two later. But since breakfasting *chez* Arlott I have seized on any chance to drink those few bottles of Private Cuvée (like Grande Cuvée, non-vintage dated, but very definitely a champagne *de luxe*) which remain undrunk.

The wine had all the refreshment of any good champagne, all fizz and head-clearing steeliness, but it also had the weight that characterized Private Cuvée and can still be found in some Krug vintages (and also most notably in some of the wines of Bollinger, Alfred Gratien and Roederer). This combination of creaminess and body meant that the wine blithely took on — a large platter of kippers. I love kippers and always used to ask for them as a special pre-festive Christmas Eve treat, but with tea, lots of it. I would never normally counsel drinking wine of any sort with such an oily, salty, breakfasty food but, if the circumstances are right and the wine is good enough, champagne and kippers can be one of life's memorable experiences.

CHAPTER TWO
A PRE-PRANDIAL BRACER
FINO & MANZANILLA SHERRY
'Oh, what a pleasure it is to have a good appetite, when you know that an excellent meal is waiting for you!' BRILLAT-SAVARIN, LA PHYSIOLOGIE DU GOUT

Anyone who spends more than ten minutes in Andalucia, the languorous southern tip of Spain, will find it hard to accept the well-documented fact that only a third as much sherry is drunk in Spain as in Britain.

In Jerez, Sanlucar de Barrameda and Puerto de Santa

Maria — which are to sherry what Reims, Epernay and Ay are to champagne — sherry seems to be as vital to the innards of the locals as air is to the rest of us. And since one of the wonders of the wine world happens to be a local speciality, so are bibulous homilies to celebrate that fact. The visitor is assured that if he refuses one before eleven, he'll have to drink eleven before one. Once one *copita* has been drained, then only a second will stop him walking with a limp. And a third? Well, he must understand that each *copita* is merely *la penultima*.

The sherry most typically drunk in the shade of Jerez's jacarandas and in the headily maritime atmosphere of Sanlucar's and Puerto's shellfish bars is Fino, or its even more delicate Sanlucar cousin, Manzanilla. The locals know that this sort of sherry, the lightest, driest and tangiest, is the most difficult to make, and revere it accordingly. Those of us raised in the UK, which has so obligingly absorbed huge quantities of Jerez's less refined produce, blended and sweetened into commercial Amontillados and Creams, would do well to follow their example.

Sherry, in Fino or Manzanilla form, is the ideal aperitif for the gastronomically aware and even, in what one hopes are exceptional circumstances, the ever-so-slightly sated. It may seem perverse to start a book about combining food and wine by recommending a wine to savour on its own, but surely the first essential for enjoyment of any meal, however simple, is a sharpened or restored appetite.

The job of an aperitif, as Latin scholars and Italian students will know, is to open something, in this case us, to the sensory pleasures ahead. A glass of Fino or, especially, Manzanilla, acts on the appetite rather like a brisk walk by the sea. Someone should measure the ozone content of these wines. Their pungent, dry tanginess seems to act as a starting pistol on the gastric juices, whatever the circumstances, provided of course that the wine itself is in good condition. In Andalucia this is rarely a problem. Although Finos and Manzanillas are very delicate, having been brought up like Victorian schoolgirls sheltered from fresh air and sunlight, back home they are usually sold, and robustly consumed, by the half-bottle so that no wine is left prey to the fast-fade effect of oxygen.

Exported Finos and Manzanillas usually come in standard-sized bottles however and often seem, understandably, to lack some of the vigour of samples sipped by the

FINOS*MANZANILLAS

back door of a *bodega*. They need careful handling for maximum appreciation. They should be served chilled, and finished up as soon as possible — within a day or two of opening if the freshness that is the major part of their appeal is not to evaporate. These are wines for big households or big drinkers. Any leftovers are best preserved in the fridge, having been stoppered as soon as possible, preferably in a smaller bottle, to allow minimum fraternizing between wine and air. (This is how most wine leftovers, and certainly any aromatic wine designed for early consumption, is best kept if it must be kept; the less air there is in the bottle, the slower the wine's decline.)

Gonzalez Byass's Tio Pepe is perhaps the finest Fino, made in enormous quantity. La Guita and Barbadillo's Solear are two of Sanlucar's most respected Manzanillas. And Puerto Finos, especially that of Osborne, have a softness that appeals to many. But the sherries that are perhaps most intellectually satisfying are those culled from one of the Almacenistas, or ancient storehouses of top quality wine, on which the firm of Emilio Lustau have trained a much-needed spotlight.

In case you're beginning to wonder, this is by no means a food-free chapter. The inevitable consequence of the twin facts that Jerezanos drink an awful lot of Fino and that Fino makes you extremely hungry is that they treat themselves to some of the most handsome pre-prandial snacks in the world — *tapas*. These mouthfuls deserve an audience far outside Spain, especially now that we live in an era when nibbling, or 'grazing', has considerable public approval.

Who could ask for more of a summer lunch than a bottle of Fino or Manzanilla and a thoughtful collection of *tapas*? Salted almonds, warm and glistening straight from the pan, are an Andalucian favourite in the autumn, their harvest roughly coinciding with the vintage, or *vendimia*. The sweet, fatty local raw ham, called *jamon serrano*, is eaten all year round in irregular slices of glistening crimson hacked from huge chunks of uncompromising-looking flesh. Then there's *lomo*, slices of pork fillet macerated in oil and red peppers so that it is orange and tart, like the spicy *chorizo* sausages that are also chopped up to punctuate mouthfuls of Fino.

Top quality, genuinely fruity green olives are perhaps the easiest of all *tapas* to provide outside Spain, but the crisp and juicy deep-fried strips of green pepper would require no specialist shopping. They could easily be made at the same time as a batch of the deep-fried, breadcrumbed blobs of thick cheese sauce so frequently served in Jerez. As a flavouring ingredient of this, Cheddar represents a distinct improvement on the local cheese, also served in cubes as *tapas*. *Tortilla*, that adaptable baked omelette-cum-savoury cake, is a staple in many parts of Spain and in sherry country tends to be chopped into cubes so as to conform to the convention that, like other *tapas*, it can be eaten with nothing more complicated than a mouth and fingers. Left whole, a *tortilla* could transform — cosmetically at least — a collection of *tapas* from a snack into a meal. Cubed, cooked potatoes, slowly sautéed onions and eggs are the only essential constituents.

In Jerez and particularly the two seaside sherry towns, a high proportion of *tapas* are based on fish: succulent shellfish of all sizes and all shades of pink, orange and grey, marinated fresh anchovies, or sardines grilled, stuffed and curled on to sticks. Morecambe Bay shrimps may sound less exotic, but would make no less a complement, and compliment, to a self-respecting Fino.

What almost all these things (I hesitate to call them 'dishes') have in common is salt. Is it perhaps the tang, the almost briny quality, so characteristic of Fino and Manzanilla that sets the tongue on edge in quest of a more solid reminder of the sea?

CHAPTER THREE

AN UNEXPECTED PLEASURE
TARAMASALATA & ZINFANDEL
'It was inconceivable that a wine from California would have anything to say to a cultivated European gentleman beyond some straightforward advice about vaginal hygiene, sanitised lavatory seats and the rest of it.' AUBERON WAUGH, WAUGH ON WINE

Look, this may sound crazy — even revolting — but let me assure you, it is delicious.

There are all sorts of non-traditional foods, which I suppose means not British and not French, now eaten with great frequency in Britain but given scant attention in the standard texts on food and wine. *Taramasalata*, that oily paste of cured grey mullet roe or — much more commonly in this country — smoked cod's roe, is one of them. It varies from a fair imitation of a heavily salted synthetic strawberry cream to an almost acridly authentic smoked fish purée.

One night we were attempting to remedy a local short-term glut of some of the finest *taramasalata* known to man, one of the particularly acrid sort made at London's answer to Manhattan's finest, the Rosslyn Delicatessen. I don't think it was anything as logical as the American connection that made me open a bottle of Ridge Zinfandel to drink with it. Nor could I claim the spirit of gastro-academic enquiry formed any part of my motivation. If I were asked to describe in one word why I chose that particular wine, the word would have to be 'greed'. I just felt like seeing what that bottle tasted like, and I didn't care too much that what I happened to be eating with it hardly leapt to mind as the wine's natural partner. Does this sound a familiar method of menu-planning?

In short, this exciting pairing of the edible and the drinkable was discovered in the most common way of all — by complete chance.

Ridge Zinfandels need a word of explanation. Turning their backs on the slightly hot, sometimes jammy, berry-flavoured models that are typical of 'the California grape' (now known to have set down its roots in the heel of Italy), Ridge give Zinfandel the *cru classé* treatment. They buy top quality, concentrated grapes produced by very old vines in the hills of western California, leach lots of colour and tannin out of them and put them into small oak casks to make them taste even more tannic and essence-like in youth.

The specimen that went so beautifully with our *tarama* leftovers was only four years old and still extremely high in mouth-puckering tannins, but it seemed to be precisely this element that took on so readily the smoke in the *tarama*. And perhaps it was the intensity of the smoky flavour in the food that distracted from the strength of the tannin so that the goal of any wine and food conjunction was achieved: the food made the wine taste better and vice versa.

This tannin and smoke theory sounded good, but a bit unconvincing, till I happened to try, much more recently, the more ethnically intact combination of *mozzarella in carrozza* using smoked mozzarella, which had a very similar note to the Rosslyn *taramasalata*, and Ceretto's Barolo Bricco Asili 1980. Again, the wine was dense, concentrated, almost murky, and very tannic. Again, the combination worked most flatteringly for each party.

15

Allow me to present, therefore, the following gastro-hypothesis: that a young purple brute of a wine will taste softer and less brutish if drunk with something quite heavily smoked. (Though note that straight smoked fish would be unlikely to work particularly well since tannin tends to make fish taste metallic. See the next chapter for some ideas on what to drink with smoked fish.)

CHAPTER FOUR
SMOKED FISH, SWEET WINE
BERRY BROS LUNCH
'For king-like rolls the Rhine,
And the scenery's divine,
And the victuals and the wine
Rather good.'
CHARLES STUART CALVERLEY, DOVER TO MUNICH

Smoked fish — salmon, then trout and now mackerel, eel, even marlin — that popular and labour-saving first course, conventionally rings alarm bells for arbiters of what to drink with what. The fish is strongly flavoured, being relatively pungent, salty and, often, fairly oily. This means that it calls for a wine with lots of character. A good Gewurztraminer from Alsace (so often a little oily itself) has been the traditional accompaniment to platefuls of boardroom smoked salmon. The match works well and I had always assumed it was the high alcohol of the Gewurz that gave it the guts to stand up for itself in such powerful company. A lunch at Berry Bros. & Rudd suggested another possible explanation.

The premises of Berry Bros. at 3 St James's Street, London SW1 must be the most atmospheric of any wine merchant in the world, if we discount those of gnarled *paysans* who sell direct from picturesque cellar doors. Berry's have been at that address since 1732 and the miracle is that no bright spark has been allowed to modernize the premises. The ground-floor sales office is still a low-ceilinged, bare-boarded chamber with not a price tag, and hardly even a bottle, in sight. Orders are taken by well-spoken chaps at tall, ancient desks who, it comes as some surprise to note, do not use quill pens.

This room still houses one of London's first weighing machines, and ledgers recording the weights of early customers, such as Beau Brummel and Byron. Below this are cellars, still very much in use, and above is a suite of well-restored panelled dining-rooms with a William Morris fire-

16

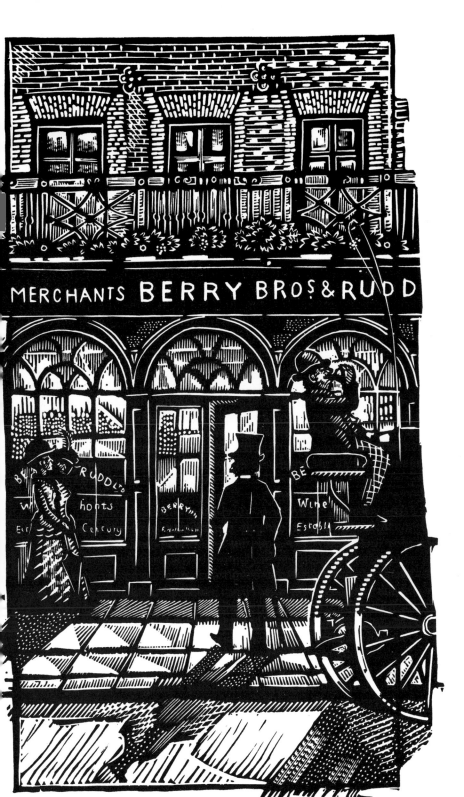

place and yards of William De Morgan tiles in perfect condition. Just across the gentlemen and taxis of St James's Street is another wine merchant, Justerini & Brooks, a parvenu outfit founded in 1749, which, like Berry's, owes its survival to the success in the US of the house brand of Scotch whisky. There is much crossing of the street for mutual competitive lunching by the directors of the two companies, but I got my invitation into the Berry dining-room on the basis of being a wine writer.

It was the first course that was so instructive. Backed by two and a half centuries (curiously under-played back in 1982) of wine lore, Berry's chose to serve with strongly smoked trout the most gorgeous mature hock: Hochheimer Kirchenstück Riesling Spätlese 1976 from one of the Rheingau's most sumptuous estates, Aschrott'sche. I would have thought that this wine, probably only about 9 per cent alcohol (as opposed to 12 or 13 per cent in many Alsace Gewurztraminers), might have been overwhelmed by the strongly flavoured fish. Not a bit of it.

The deep golden wine, probably at its peak at ten years old from the slightly low-acid vintage of 1976, was still distinctly sweet but the acid sufficiently high to make the finish of the wine decidedly refreshing. No turgid cloy here. Instead it had developed that intense, arrestingly high-toned scent of a mature Riesling, the smell likened by some to 'petrol' or 'kerosene', for want of any better word. Perhaps this substituted for the 'oiliness' of Gewurz? It was a wine at the height of its power and would have been delicious drunk on its own, but the combination was truly inspiring. Doubtless part of the explanation was the magic of sweet and salt so well sung in port and Stilton, or even that other standby first course, Parma ham and melon. However, it's no good putting any old sweet wine with smoked fish. It has to have good acid too to be sufficiently appetizing for the first part of a meal, and it has to have real character, derived either from such a distinctive (and apparently 'sweet') grape variety as Gewurztraminer, or from the sort of complexity that only first-rate Riesling locked into glass for a decade or so will develop.

CHAPTER FIVE

LIQUID WITH LIQUID
WINE & SOUP

'But a glass of wine after soup is, as the French say, the verre de santé. The current of opinion sets in favour of Hock: but I am for Madeira; I do not fancy Hock till I have laid a substratum of Madeira.' THOMAS LOVE PEACOCK, CROTCHET CASTLE

There's soup that needs a wine with it, soup that doesn't, and soup that *is* wine. In fact, now I come to think of it, an embarrassingly high proportion of my favourite soups fall into this last category.

One of them is the simplest of thin onion broths in which sliced and gently stewed onions are stretched into a soup by a simmer with water and an everyday Alsace, such as Pinot Blanc, before being used blatantly as a vehicle for a grilled, cheese-topped *croûte*. Then there's the sybarite's version of Jewish penicillin — chicken soup — just the juice leached from a chicken carcass, a few carrots and onions or leeks after an hour or two's simmer in some bone-dry white wine, diluted to reduce the acidity. And there's no need to bid farewell to wine-based soups for the summer either. I love my adaptation of Hungarian cherry soup in which a pound of cherries, the more bitterly characterful the better, are stoned, slightly stewed, cooled and mixed with sour cream or *crème fraîche*, lemon zest, a little sugar, cinnamon, a measure of brandy and a whole bottle of aromatic dry white wine. (I have come across no Hungarian white outside Hungary that is suitable for this extraordinarily self-indulgent potion, though almost any Alto Adige white would be ideal.)

In common with these wine-based soups, probably the majority of other soups are best enjoyed as food and drink in one. Certainly I find a bowlful or mug of hot soup the perfect antidote to over-enthusiastic wine consumption. London's wine merchants regularly pump thousands of pounds into the coffers of City caterers such as Ring & Brymer for groaning boards of artfully sliced meats and mass-hashed salads in order to refresh their guests after big tastings. I'd be so much better restored by a simple cauldron of *potage bonne femme* and some good bread. But I digress.

The main purpose of this chapter is to put in a small plea for the almost extinct custom of drinking old-fashioned fortified wines with old-fashioned soups, by which I mean clear soups and consommés. They fell from favour in the Sixties, perhaps because they were classified with Brown Windsor soup as too British to satisfy our new love affair with things which were then called Continental. But by the end of 1986 I thought I could just discern their renaissance in fashion-conscious restaurants, perhaps partly a result of the increasing Japanese influence on what we eat. Long may this trend continue, for there is something miraculously satisfying about these carefully made essences.

I sadly suspect that it will be even more difficult to persuade the British public back to their traditional wine partners, Madeira and nut-dark sherries of real quality, such as well-aged dry Amontillado and dry Oloroso. Far more than such fashionable drinks as white burgundy and Perrier water, these are actually part of our national heritage — drinks created by and for the British and shipped to these shores by our seafaring ancestors. Somehow we've lost our taste for them, and I suspect it is our wariness of their distinguishing mark, the characteristic described so beautifully in the 'Pardoner's Tale' by Chaucer, one of our most literate sons of the wine trade, as their 'fumositée'.

Very fumos indeed are these old-fashioned fortified wines, the sort that newcomers to wine might describe distastefully as 'a bit strong'. It is presumably this curious and complex smell (burnt, in the case of a good Madeira; pungently nutty, in the case of fine dark sherries), and the extra alcohol (about 18 per cent as opposed to an average of 11 per cent in unfortified wines), that gives them the strength to stand up to the powerfully pure scent of a good consommé.

I can visualize, though have never, alas, experienced, the ideal union of the two elements under discussion here. The piping hot liquid, limpid mahogany, would arrive (note that 'arrive' — I'm eating, not cooking, in my fantasy), presaged by a cloud of compellingly savoury vapour, in a two-handled cup of finest white English china with the most discreet figuring on it. A Madeira, Sercial or Verdelho, from a century-old solera, tawny but winking greenish-yellow at the rim, is served in a bubbly old rummer, almost dangerous in the irregularity of its base. Here we have a thorough hotchpotch of different periods, but an assembly of aspects of British history to warm the heart and soul as well as the body and brain.

CHAPTER SIX
LUNCH CHEZ LEVY
GALLIA TOGATA & CHEVRE

'There comes a time of life when one begins to prize young wine.' COLETTE, PRISONS ET PARADIS

Everyone I know who has a cellar, whether it be a couple of cardboard boxes under the stairs or a magnificent suite of interlocking bunkers, loses track of what they have in it. (Everyone, that is, except Edmund Penning-Rowsell, the most generous of hosts and most meticulous of record-keepers.)

Paul Levy is no exception to this rule. During a weekend at his Cotswold retreat we went below on a dig through the icy stone cavern which houses his collection of bottles. He dimly remembered that the sommelier at the Ancona hotel, which had had the pleasure of receiving the Levy family on holiday several years previously, had pressed a collection of local wines into his hand baggage, on condition that they were shared with me. They had to be found.

The search involved a lot of awkward manoeuvring round the wooden cases in the cellar's 'in-tray' and the forlorn collections of upright bottles that were obviously in some metaphorical pending tray. Bottle after bottle was pulled out, only to be pushed back in either smug anticipation or mystified impatience. After many a false scent, we found the Ancona Collection, the major part of which, delightful as it had doubtless once been, was probably not designed for languishing beneath Cotswold cobwebs.

One bottle, however, was an absolute plum, and an unexpected joy with the first course of our Sunday lunch — if shamefully obscure to this brace of wine writers. You know how it is once you wander off the well-marked path of familiar wines — especially in Mediterranean wineland where the signposts are so few and far between. The label offers an assortment of equally unfamiliar proper names. Is it a place? Is it a grape? Is it human? Gallia Togata 1973, said this one, promising 16 degrees of alcohol from the Fattoria di Montesecco. We had not a clue what to expect, and Burton Anderson between hardcovers was further away than the corkscrew.

It was an extraordinary wine, coppery coloured and sweet, almost burnt caramel at first, carrying through a distinctly almondy flavour with fullness and richness, to a clean, dry finish. This was a real beginning, middle and end sort of wine, brimming with self-confidence, worried not a jot — and quite rightly — that it was being received in ignorance and belying any attempt to classify it. It comes from Pesaro — a place I always associate with pedalos because of a previous incarnation as holiday brochure compiler — which is sandwiched between Sangiovese di Romagna and Verdicchio country. However, the wine tasted like nothing from either area. A reflection chiefly of the under-appreciated Malvasia grape, and treated to oak and bottle age, it is made by just one producer, Massimo Schiavi so, like so many of Italy's more fascinating wines, has no official status.

While I was drooling over this wonder, Paul was collecting another one from his Aga — a goat's cheese soufflé as prescribed by Alice Waters of Berkeley's Chez Panisse in Northern California, the world's smartest campus diner. It was toasted and puffy on top and creamy and runny in the middle. Here again, the contained sweetness of the wine was the perfect foil for the saltiness of the first course.

Italy is full of these arcane treats. Where there's a half-decent wine maker, there's an inspiringly distinct sort of wine for the world's delectation — if only the world would take notice.

CHAPTER SEVEN
ENOTRIA INCOGNITA
VERSATILE ITALIAN REDS
'There is something nice and matey about a good bottle of wine.' CHARLES WALTER BERRY, IN SEARCH OF WINE

Like any halfway sensitive Briton, I love Italy, and feel a particular affection for Tuscany. It's so unequivocally beautiful (and so stuffed with expatriate English-speakers) that it feels somehow as easy to understand as to appreciate. In matters gastronomic this is not necessarily the case.

My first intimation of the size of the gulf that yawns between the eating and drinking habits of the British and the Italians came about twenty-four hours after leaving school. It was a very straight high school for girls in Cumbria at which there was no nonsense about devoting any attention to what went into our digestive systems. The consequence was that just about all I could bear to ingest of school meals was water and salt. The night I left school I took a bus to London,

then a train to Livorno, then a clattering little carriage called a '*direttissimo*' to a spot on the south Tuscan coast on to which clings one of the world's smarter hotels. I was to spend the summer as chambermaid to the likes of Paul Getty Jr. and Charlie Chaplin (met in his underpants on my first morning — my fault for not understanding 'don't come in' in Italian) earning £4 a week. (It wasn't all *that* long ago — the hotel just paid very badly.) So emaciated had I become from my school diet that I was immediately christened La Grissina (the breadstick) by the rest of the staff, mostly locals. It was also broken to me that at staff meals, the focus of this new life below stairs, I could drink as much wine as I liked, but if I wanted any drinking water I'd have to pay for it. That had them going at home in Kirkandrews-on-Eden.

Since then I have selflessly exposed myself to Italian wine and food in all its proudly regional glory and come to love it, perhaps even more than French cuisine, for its robust and healthy simplicity, but there are still shocks. None of these was ruder than when, on a freezing spring night in Tuscany, I ordered, at some cost, the new broad beans with local cheese on the menu, foolishly licking my lips at the prospect of a little terracotta dish bubbling with baby beans covered in melted cheese. What I got, as the rest of the party fell, hooting unkindly, on their steaming *ribollita*, was a small slice of virgin cheese and a pile of broad beans *in their pods*. I'm all for an elemental style of presentation but isn't this dish (famous, I later learnt to my chagrin) taking protest against processed foods a bit far? This sort of thing may go down very well in Tuscany, but I can't see it ever catching on in Torquay.

The burghers of Torquay, and their countrymen, would be well advised to take more notice of Italian wines, however. The country was, after all, known by the Greeks, no mean winemakers themselves, as Enotria, or the land of wine. Its location and landscape, and therefore wine potential, has not changed since then. Italy produces more wine than any other country by quite a margin, and the determined enthusiast can winkle out of it a far wider range of good quality wines than are made anywhere else, including France. The problem for the British wine drinker is that there has been a distinct shortage of determined enthusiasts to do the winkling for him. But now we are at last starting to see a wider variety of fine Italian wines in this country and I, for one, hope that the new generation of winklers will give due attention to a category of wine in which Italy excels: light- to medium-bodied, soft but appetizing reds designed

24

to be drunk young with food. Francophiles might see them as Italy's answer to Beaujolais, but most of the better examples tend to have an extra, appetite-honing ingredient, a perceptible bite, bordering on bitterness.

Chianti, the staple and exasperatingly variable red of Tuscany, can exhibit these qualities, and is certainly — when well made — designed specifically for the table. But the wines that more reliably demonstrate a happy partnership with a wide range of savoury foods are the much juicier likes of Dolcetto, Bonarda and even the lowly Barbera from the north-western regions of Piedmont and Oltrepo' Pavese. I can imagine few supper dishes based on meat or cheese which would remain unenhanced by a bottle of young Bonarda or Barbera from the Fugazza sisters of the Castello di Luzzano due south of Milan in Lombardy. These frank, honest, early-maturing juices constitute just the style of wine to wash down a creamy pasta dish or oniony *pissaladière*. They brim over with the same sort of basic vigour as Italian food — the sort of food served in Italy, that is, not the miserable permutations of mozzarella, tomato, mushrooms and veal served in the name of Italy in British *trattorie*.

Barbera is one of the world's most planted grape varieties and deserves to have a much better reputation. Dolcetto, altogether a beefier grape variety, but with just the same sort of easy gulpability, could also do with greater recognition outside Enotria. I reckon this will happen as we slowly come to realize that it is unreasonable to expect every wine to behave like a classed growth claret.

CHAPTER EIGHT
SAUCISSON IN BEAUJOLAIS
JULIENAS & AUJAS
'Burgundy is always a man's wine; Beaujolais has a more feminine grace. Burgundy graces the table of the Guards; no Light Infantryman need be ashamed of Beaujolais.' MAURICE HEALY, STAY ME WITH FLAGONS

There is, of course, a world of difference between a stereotype and an archetype. The sort of Frenchman who appears in advertisements for cross-Channel ferries and mass-market Brie is a stereotype. Ernest Aujas on the other hand (who also wears a beret) is an archetype — an archetypal French *paysan* who, to my immense satisfaction, could not be recreated by even the most extravagantly paid account executive working with the most imaginative art director and most sensitive costume designer.

It would be impossible for them to find a face as memorably etched into an expression of sceptical fortitude as the Aujas one has been by daily exposure to the elements for well over fifty vintages in the Beaujolais hills. Nor could they possibly find such a convincingly worn set of (once) bright *bleus de travail* which constitute the French workman's uniform, simulated stress being no substitute for a decade or two of cellar work. And they certainly wouldn't dream of glueing on to a bottom lip the dog-end that is Ernest Aujas's trademark.

Monsieur Aujas is both inimitable and utterly admirable. He lives in an uncompromisingly functional house centred on a tiny kitchen just outside the village of Juliénas (whose 'S', in the perverse local ways of rural France, is not pronounced, while that of Aujas is). Any worthwhile wine from the steep, granitic vineyards of the nine top villages or *crus* in the north of the Beaujolais region is considered more serious and worthy of ageing than the juicy young wines for early gulping that are the norm for basic Beaujolais, or even the superior Beaujolais-Villages. The wines of Juliénas in particular are renowned for their vigour and texture. But such are the traditions inherited by Ernest Aujas that his wines are even more substantial and *sérieux* than is usual for his native village.

He picks his grapes according to their ripeness rather than by the calendar, some years risking almost zero production as a result of autumn storms. His wine is still slowly bubbling in the ancient fermentation vats long after the last bottle of Beaujolais Nouveau has been flogged off in the wine bars of London and liquor stores of New York. They're then kept in oak, a material of which 99 per cent of Beaujolais produced today is blissfully ignorant, before the complicated business of bottling *chez* Aujas.

He won't touch the wines when anything important is happening in the vineyard. They react in sympathy during budding, flowering or ripening, apparently. Nor does he approve of the upset caused by the *vent du Midi* either, and according to his forebears the moon also influences the stability of the wine. He and his wife will bottle therefore, by hand, only when the wind is in the north and the moon is on the wane. And he insists on labelling all the cartons by hand too. His British importer, a Norfolk farmer well versed in the stately pace of agricultural life, has come to dread receiving a large order for an Aujas wine.

A tour of the Aujas cellars does not take long, and the extent of his domain is barely ten acres, which means that within an hour of arrival favoured visitors (such as the film crew with which I encountered the Aujas phenomenon) can be experiencing one of the world's gastronomic highs: *rosette de Lyons* and *cru* Beaujolais.

Madame urged us into the modest Aujas *salon* towards noon, suggesting purposefully that we spared a moment to *casse* a *croûte* with her and her husband. Once the dozen or so of us had been squeezed round the plastic tablecloth, and had refocused our eyes according to the demands of the wallpaper, she set to breaking crusts with a vengeance. Thick *baguettes* were first squeezed and then noisily cracked open under the repeated application of her cleaver to their crusty carapaces. Close inspection of their consistency should be compulsory for any student baker in this country.

The bread was passed round and inelegantly torn apart while the cleaver got to work on a fat, grey, lumpen cylinder, transforming it into glistening slices of coarse *saucisson*, salty, fatty, garlicky and a not dissimilar colour to the crimson edge of the 1983 Juliénas Monsieur Aujas was pouring into generous-sized glasses.

At that moment it was impossible to imagine a more satis-

fying combination of the edible and potable than that particular specimen of local *charcuterie* and the equally meaty
Beaujolais. No, no lunch, the crew assured the producer,
munching and gulping as though possessed. For a snack to
make an ACTT member forgo what is his by right and years
of negotiation, it has to be pretty damn good. It was.

The combined concentrating forces of traditional vinifi-
cation and as good a summer as 1983 were clearly enough to
add to Beaujolais's naturally high acidity the opulence of extra fruit, and even a little bit of tannin, which would keep
this wine going well into the 1990s if required and possible.
Here was a wine, assaulted by us in 1986, which would perform that magical *cru* Beaujolais trick of starting to taste like
a red burgundy about seven years after it was made. I have
tasted Moulin-à-Vent made at the Château des Jacques in the
1940s which had achieved this state beatifically.

The Aujas wine's acidity and opulent fruitiness flattered
the juicy saltiness of the *saucisson*, cutting the fat nicely so
that it became impossible to take a sip of wine without immediately re-checking this agreeable hypothesis, and equally
impossible to chew a slice of *rosette* without slaking one's
thirst straightaway.

We reeled out, having tried his '81 and his burgundian
wonder of a '76, well after one o'clock, realizing only as we
left that we had been keeping the Aujas family from their
déjeuner or, to be literal about the French for lunch, the
breaking of their fast.

CHAPTER NINE
RED WINES WITH FISH

'When thirsty grief in wine we steep,
When healths and draughts go free,
Fishes, that tipple in the deep,
Know no such liberty.'
RICHARD LOVELACE, TO ALTHEA, FROM PRISON

At last the palates of the world are being liberated from the
tyranny of the silly 'red wines with meat, white wines with
fish' rule.

This diktat is notoriously fallible, not to say utterly break-
able, and is merely a crude way of expressing some gener-
alities about food and wine. Of course, matching wine with
food depends on factors much more subtle than mere colour.

You have only to think of how often red and white wines are confused by blindfold tasters to realize that. As outlined in the introduction, the most important determining factor is to match the 'weight' of the food with the 'body' of the wine. Because meat dishes *tend* to be a bit heavier than ones based on fish, and because there are (just) more full-bodied reds than full-bodied whites, red wines have for decades been recommended, blanket fashion, with meat.

The white wine and fish rule is based on a similar generality. Most fish is improved by a dash of acidity, hence its being served with a squeeze of lemon juice or wine-based *fumet*. Because, in very general terms, white wines *tend* to have slightly higher, or at least more noticeable acid than reds, white wines have diligently been recommended with fish.

In northern Portugal and Galicia, that starkly beautiful area of Spain which abuts and echoes it, they would laugh at the idea that red wine should not be drunk with fish. There the inhabitants guzzle inordinate quantities of some of the finest shellfish in the world, together with some of the sharp, eye-wateringly dry, almost fizzy red versions of Vinho Verde. It is surely only their conditioning, not their palates, that are different to ours.

This is not to say that all red wines would be delicious with all fish. A young Châteauneuf-du-Pape would be pretty disgusting with Dover sole in almost any circumstances, I would have thought. Most wines high in tannin, which means most young red wines designed for ageing, such as most serious Bordeaux and Rhône reds and some red burgundies, are unhappy with the average fish. There is something about fish, white fish in particular, that makes the wine taste metallic.

Very simply cooked, especially delicate fish probably *is* better with the pure flattery of a dry white wine, but salmon is an obvious partner for a light, low-tannin red. Other fish with the flavour and texture to stand up particularly well to reds (and rosés) include brill, halibut, John Dory, monkfish, red mullet, salmon trout and turbot. Fillets and escalopes of such fish are now regularly served in sauces based on red wine in the world's less traditional restaurants.

Reds that will most enhance the relative delicacy and subtlety of most fish dishes served in Britain are those that are low in tannin and body and refreshingly high in acidity.

A fairly light Beaujolais (probably not M. Aujas's Juliénas) would be the obvious choice, as would any other well-made wine based on the Gamay grape. (These are thin on the ground but little pockets of vineyard in the Rhône hinterland can produce such goodies as a fine Gamay de l'Ardèche.)

Most Cabernet Sauvignon-based wines are difficult because of their high tannin content, but the Cabernet Franc grape can yield many a Chinon, Bourgueil, Saumur-Champigny or even Anjou Rouge, which work well with positively sauced fish. Lightish Pinot Noir-based wines, such as red burgundies of simple status and/or an unripe year and red Sancerre can also make very pretty companions indeed to fish. The bargain basement way to enjoy red wine with fish is to drink a typical red Vin de Pays with it. The carbonic maceration principle of whole-berry fermentation which results in very soft, low-tannin wines prevails in the Midi, and the wines tend to be rather light and a bit tart because they are made from fairly productive vines — ideal fish wines and, significantly, some of the most difficult red wines to distinguish blind from white.

Italy can also supply a bevy of light, soft red wines to wash down more substantial fish dishes. True Valpolicella and, particularly, Bardolino, are virtually *vins du lac* anyway, but there is also a host of wines made in the far alpine north of the country, the Trentino-Alto Adige, based on the Schiava grape. Very young, very simple, very healthy Tuscan reds (the sort that once filled *fiaschi* of Chianti) could also do the trick.

Many pink wines come into their own in a fish context, though with a fairly grand dish the rosé should have some delicacy and refinement. A good Sancerre Rosé perhaps, or a Rosé de Marsannay.

CHAPTER TEN

GOURMANDISE AT YQUEM
'Gourmandism is by no means unbecoming in women.'
BRILLAT-SAVARIN, LA PHYSIOLOGIE DU GOUT

In July 1986 I received a very puzzling invitation. The time and place were clear enough. I was bid for 11 a.m. on 30 September to Château d'Yquem, indisputably the greatest property in Sauternes, the sweet wine district south-east of Bordeaux The host was quite plain too: Herr Hardy Rodenstock, perhaps the most famous of a new group of near-fanatical fine wine collectors in Germany. But *what* exactly was I being invited to?

In the English part of the trilingual invitation, it was described simply as a 'wine tasting with rare wines' which 'will end at about 10 p.m.' I was told to wear a metaphorical black tie, that my invitation was for one person only and was not transferable, and that I should reply, by registered post, by 30 August. I reckoned that any event to which a typical German postman should not be relied upon to convey my acceptance would probably be worth going to. I was right.

The 'wine tasting with rare wines' turned out to be a twelve-course meal to which forty of us sat down at about noon on Tuesday and from which we got up at one o'clock on Wednesday morning. We were each served *sixty-six* different wines, not to taste — that would have been easy — but to *drink*. There was not a spittoon in sight, until about eight o'clock in the evening when Michael Broadbent, Christie's 'Mr Wine' (under whose hammer a good proportion of all that we enjoyed must have passed a time or two), finally secured a rather grand-looking *cache-pot* for himself and his neighbours. Around 3500 splinter-stemmed crystal glasses were, in sobering progression, cleaned, filled, emptied, and cleaned again. Thank heavens I stopped myself, at the last minute, wearing a new skin-tight frock. The seams would never have withstood the strain. As luck would have it, I wore indulgently elastic black on that exquisite autumn morning. There was more than a hint of Glyndebourne as we foregathered on the lawns in front of the château, our shamelessly sophisticated clothing somehow at odds with the natural beauty of the setting.

Château d'Yquem is in a commanding position, both literally and figuratively, in this almost archaically rural corner of France. The fortified *château-fermier* stands on Sauternes' only hilltop and from under its spreading cedars we could see row upon row of world-famous vines stretching through the crisp sunshine into the smoky blue distance, patiently awaiting the development of the 'noble rot' that makes great sweet wines even greater and sweeter by attacking them, concentrating the sugar and flavour elements. This was the crucial time of year for the umpteenth-generation guardian of Château d'Yquem, Comte Alexandre de Lur-Saluces, who was waiting to see whether, now that he had a vineyard full of ripe, healthy grapes, the succeeding mists of autumn would favour the spread of this magical fungus. (It did.)

He didn't look too worried. After all, however noble he may be himself, at Yquem he is, *au fond*, a farmer, and has to adopt the farmer's philosophical attitude towards the elements. The Comtesse was there too, congratulating Hardy Rodenstock on having prised Yquem's official biographer, the American gastronomic writer Richard Olney, out of his Provençal bolthole. Most of the rest of the lip-smacking party were Hardy's impressively experienced fellow collectors from Germany, and members of the Bordeaux vinocracy, such as Messieurs Dourthe, Mähler-Besse and Jean-François Moueix, Jacques Hébrard of Château Cheval Blanc, Thierry Manoncourt of Château Figeac and Baron Philippe de Rothschild's grandson Philippe playing hookey from business school.

Michael Broadbent and I represented Britain, the avid Dutch wine collector Dr Jan Dirk Taams represented the Netherlands and a wine fanatic cum nuclear physicist I'd met at an amazing testing of '59 clarets he'd once organized in London, Bipin Desai, had flown in from Los Angeles for the event. What would this tasting be like, I asked him. 'The theme is "Hardy",' he smiled. 'He mixes things up. Everything is very casual, very understated. He buys wines to *drink*. I don't think there's been any personality of his kind in the history of wine before. He holds a special tasting like this every year. This is the first one outside Germany, but each one escalates. We all first tasted 1921 Pétrus in Munich. Today we'll have it magnum next to '21 Cheval Blanc.'

At this stage the two chefs needed to fuel us through the forthcoming marathon, Rolf-Dieter Jung of the Restaurant Fuente in Mülheim and Francis Garcia of Bordeaux's Restaurent Clavel, came out into the sunshine to give us, literally, a taste of what was to come (their whites already smelt of complex reductions). They'd arrived at 5 a.m. and couldn't stop themselves saying *bonsoir*. Since the château is uninhabited (the Lur-Saluces live in Bordeaux), the poor old kitchen must have suffered the shock of its life that day.

We filed into the château past an easel on to which a copy of the poster-sized menu had been pinned. Those of us who examined it had the curious sensation of feeling our stomachs churn as our palates salivated. Surely they couldn't mean to give us every one of those 16 vintages of Ygrec, the mind-blowingly alcoholic dry wine of Yquem? And a blind tasting of ten clarets from vintages 1937 back to 1848? Such an exercise might mean something to the likes of Hardy and his fellow Feinschmeckers, whose cellars are lined with pre-phylloxera bottles, but those of us with more limited experience of these vintages would be delighted by the unadorned chance to savour any one of these clarets in isolation. Were we really to be served *homard, langoustines, foie gras, cèpes* and *truffes* at the same meal? And what about the Yquem listed as '*c.* 1750'?

As we took our places in the light, sunny dining-room overlooking the vineyards on one side and the nicely rustic courtyard on the other, we were each presented with a splendid red-velvet-bound tasting album (whose dimensions were such as to severely hamper the quite stunning *service* over the next thirteen hours). I felt very grand at being put, in this the first of three varied *placements*, next to the Count and opposite Hardy.

The Count told me without rancour that Hardy, who is known as Herr Yquem in Germany, had tasted far more vintages of Yquem than he, the owner, had. 'He probably still owns more than me too,' he added. Then he opened his album and, looking at the title page, asked Hardy what the figure seven on it meant. 'It means it's the seventh such rare wine tasting that I have organized,' explained Hardy simply. The Count nodded glumly. 'That's what I thought it meant,' he said in a subdued sort of way.

Hardy Rodenstock could hardly be a less ostentatious character. He throws not a kilo of his modest weight about; he is merely absolutely fascinated by wine and appears to devote to it every waking minute left to him by his obviously flourishing career in the music business. It was Hardy, for instance, who acquired the much-publicized bottles of wine from the 1780s, supposedly ordered by Thomas Jefferson. He must have spent weeks organizing this extravaganza which, even the Count admitted, was not a special tasting, but a world first.

Hardy had even conducted blind water tastings to ensure that his priceless bottles were rinsed down with H_2O in its most harmonious form. (Spa waters, still and sparkling, were chosen; I must have got through several litres.)

Well, we couldn't put it off any longer. We had to get going on this marathon of consumption. A flight of four German wines was served first, including a Beerenauslese Trocken, if you please (a 'sweet dry' curiosity since banned by the German authorities), with a 'simple' salad of red mullet, artichokes and potatoes.

The *cassolette de homard aux perles de legumes* was temptingly rich for the second of a dozen courses, but the four white burgundies served with it were utterly distracting — particularly a rivetingly pure brace of Bienvenue Bâtard-Montrachets, 1979 and 1982, from André Ramonet.

Our sixteen Ygrecs followed with two more fish courses and suggested conclusively to me that this dry wine does not improve with more than ten years in bottle, but they served admirably to heighten the high point of this day-long succession of high points, a run of five vintages of Château d'Yquem, the sweet wine and no messing, that marked the end of our first session at the table. Before our sliver of fresh *foie gras* sautéed with white grapes and Yquem 1976 (it's no good describing wines as '76 in a Hardy context), we were to taste Yquem 1858, 1847, 1811 and one amazing bottle that had been put at about 1750.

Hardy, who has never disclosed exactly how or where in Paris he unearthed the Thomas Jefferson bottles, had heard that there were still some treasures from the former Tsars' cellars to be found in Leningrad. Yquem had long been a favourite with the Russian court, the Tsar having paid 20,000 gold francs for a barrel of Yquem in 1847 in one well-documented transaction. He managed to find this bottle, flask-shaped and deep indigo-coloured glass engraved all over with tiny white-painted flowers, grapes and vine leaves, as was the custom then, and marked with the arms of the Sauvage family (who did not transfer ownership of Yquem by marriage into the Lur-Saluces family till 1785).

Analysis of the glass, once Hardy had somehow spirited the bottle out of the USSR, suggested that it was mid-eighteenth century, making this wine that we were about to taste the oldest that had probably ever been tasted from a bottle. (Great sweet white wines probably stand a better

chance of survival over a few hundred years than most, and several of those present had drooled over a Thomas Jefferson bottle of Yquem 1784 at the previous year's event in Germany.)

But first we had to eat our bread and butter — and what bread and butter! The nineteenth-century Yquems, culled from cellars as far apart as Scotland and Venezuela, had turned deep tawny as very old white wines are wont to do, but tasted by no means over the hill. The 1858 was starting to be a little aggressive and the 1811 was perhaps a bit attenuated, but the 1847 was absolutely great wine, utterly alive and kicking, very vigorous, round and rich with good acid balance and a lovely long, well-integrated flavour that just went on and on.

Silence fell as the young sommelier imported from Munich tapped away at the most ancient bottle of all. Then came a communal squeal of delight as the cork emerged intact, only to crumble immediately, exhausted by the effort of preserving this wine so long. There was just one bottle, which everyone wanted to touch, enough for a good-sized glass for each of the four tables. When it was poured, it looked almost like claret, so deep-coloured and red was it. The temptation was to admire and comment, but Michael Broadbent, with the natural sense of slightly bossy responsibility that has got him where he is, reminded us sharply that this was very old wine that should be tasted immediately, before it faded.

There is no way four glasses, however beautiful (they were specially made and engraved for this particular wine by Riedel), can be shared elegantly by forty tasters, but somehow everyone managed to taste this extraordinary liquid: deep foxy red, creamy rich in texture, almost unctuous with a slight minerally edge, just starting to fall apart, but still very definitely a top quality, naturally sweet wine. What an experience, to think that we were tasting a wine made perhaps twenty years before Napoleon was even born.

The special glasses were duly auctioned for charity, the Count nobly setting a price of 12,000 francs for the first set of four. I felt sorry for Michael Broadbent who, after tasting thirty-odd wines, and making one of his extra-thorough notes on each, was expected to conduct the sale.

By now it was five in the afternoon and the golden autumn light was gently fading. We were all dying to get outside before it disappeared so, pausing only to savour the *foie gras* and 1976 Yquem, we trooped outside, the earnest ones for a tour of the cellars, the Brits for a quiet nap under a tree.

Now, I think you probably have some idea of how the rest of the day went by now. Yes, there was more of the same, only a little bit different. 'Stand-out' wines among the thirty-three that followed included Châteaux Canon 1966 from a jeroboam and Calon-Ségur 1966 from an imperial (the equivalent of six and eight bottles respectively in one); Châteaux Pétrus and Cheval Blanc in magnum, both 1921; a jeroboam of Château Mouton-Rothschild 1929 that, even at ten o'clock with Brillat-Savarin and *pain noir aux pruneaux*, was so sensationally complete it revived my flagging spirits; and two more absolutely gorgeous vintages of Château d'Yquem, 1937 and 1921.

The staff of the château and restaurants had behaved beautifully, with admirable manners and stamina throughout, but how about the guests? Since that day, a lot of people have asked me, some more politely than others, but weren't you all horribly *drunk*? And the answer, amazingly enough, is no. Funnily enough, for me and I suspect many others, the day turned into almost a battle for survival rather than an opportunity to maximize consumption. Although I consciously sipped rather than drank, I did find myself flushing down an Anadin with some Lanson 1964 at about eight o'clock (a practice which I'm sure should not be condoned on any basis). Next morning I felt eerily healthy, even when I got up at 6 a.m. to catch the red-eye special back to Heathrow. I did notice the in-flight breakfast wasn't up to much though.

CHAPTER ELEVEN
FOIE GRAS AND SAUTERNES
YQUEM & FOIE GRAS
'Sauternes are extremely sweet, although they manage to carry off the sweetness without being sickening, because of their very heavy rich body, which somehow takes the curse off so much sugar. There is no such thing as a dry Sauternes, despite the opinion of the liquor store salesman of Eighth Street, New York, who told me when I observed as much, in a highly superior tone: "We have it." '
WAVERLEY ROOT, THE FOOD OF FRANCE

My experience at Château d'Yquem, described in the previous chapter, must surely be the most extraordinary wine and food adventure I have ever had. By about halfway through this mind-boggling, liver-curdling event, roughly the *galette des cèpes au fumé des bois* stage, it became a battle to see how little we could ingest without sacrificing any one of this succession of once-in-a-lifetime experiences. Such was its marathon aspect that there were times when our bio-rhythms seemed distinctly unresponsive to the undoubted importance of the event. And yes, I suppose no one would have taken us for a busload of teetotallers as we were driven back to Bordeaux afterwards. But the extraordinary thing was that however many wines had gone before, the really, really wonderful ones, such as the Mouton-Rothschild 1929 and the Wachenheimer Goldbächer Gerümpel Trockenbee-renauslese 1937 (both served well after dark), suddenly set the pulse racing and the adrenalin flowing once more.

The main purpose of the event — if such an orgy can be said to have or need a purpose — was to taste Yquem and its dry sister, Ygrec, of various vintages. The oldest of these came in the engraved flask of Yquem dated 'circa 1750' which had been unearthed by Hardy in Leningrad. It was a wonder of preservation, though it was the 1847 that was the wonder of vivacity. Such wines are rarities indeed and were passed around to be sipped, savoured and discussed without the distraction of food. But we were given something to eat

with the final Yquem served in this first of the three sessions into which the meal had been divided. *Foie gras de canard aux raisins* soaked up the 1976, a mere babe-in-arms in this context.

Now *foie gras* and Sauternes is a combination of which the Sauternais are proud, just as they sing the justifiable praises of their wine with Roquefort. I was not utterly convinced however that our slice of fresh *foie gras* sautéed with peeled, ultra-ripe white grapes was an ideal partner for a wine as unctuous as Sauternes. Not one of life's greater problems, you may agree, but what it meant in effect was that everything on the plate and in the glass was sweet. Both the grapes and that particular vintage of Yquem were lacking the firmness a year such as 1975 could have offered, and there was none of the acidulous relief that would have been available in an accompanying salad of carefully dressed young spinach leaves or *mâche*, for instance. I didn't, naturally, tell the Count how I would have improved his menu, but resolved that next time I served *foie gras* I would make sure I didn't serve it with something too sweet.

Next time the table at Château Robinson was graced with *foie gras*, I promptly served it with something too sweet. Very clever I thought I was being, putting a half bottle of the famous, if slightly earthy, Australian answer to Yquem — De Bortoli's Noble Late Harvest Semillon 1983, made near Griffith, New South Wales — with the pot of *pâté de foie gras* from Schillinger which Johnny Hugel had so kindly sent as a Christmas present. It was a judgment on me for not lavishing our last bottle of Hugel Vendange Tardive on it. Shame on me.

Yet again, the inherent sweetness of the *foie gras*, admittedly now in less virgin form, was underlined by such a rich, sticky wine. It has won countless trophies, even against some Sauternes, and is a very well-made wine, but it just can't hide its size. At the beginning of a meal, the appetite revolts against all this unrelieved sugar. The previous year we had done the proper thing and lubricated our *pâté de foie gras* with Hugel's Riesling Vendange Tardive 1976, a wine whose sweetness is balanced by good acid and a refreshingly piercing aroma — unlike the notoriously smudgy bouquet of Semillon, the grape that the sweet wines of De Bortoli so wisely share with Sauternes.

I love the idea of something as unconventional as a sweet wine with savoury food, but I do think it needs to be served with *some*thing to relieve such concentrated sweetness, whether it be a note of sharpness in a sauce or dressing, or the saltiness of a blue cheese (see page 75).

However, I must admit that Yquem of a good year is just so sublime (and so difficult and expensive to make), that there is a good argument for giving it every ounce of attention if you're lucky enough to get your nose into it. That's certainly what I did with the almost ethereal Yquems 1937 and 1921 which were served around midnight on 30 September 1986.

At Château d'Yquem, when the Comte de Lur-Saluces is in sole charge of menu-planning, it is apparently quite usual to be served Yquem with first, main, cheese *and* sweet courses. This sort of meal sounds fascinating, though, as Richard Olney puts it, 'While such a meal is a passionate experience, it tends to leave the diner breathless.' Quite so.

CHAPTER TWELVE
IN PRAISE OF WHITE BURGUNDY
LOBSTER & MONTRACHET
'Alone in the vegetable kingdom, the vine makes the true savour of the earth intelligible to man.'
COLETTE, PRISONS ET PARADIS

Chardonnay is by now, surely, grown in every single wine-producing country – with the (just) possible exceptions of Albania, Bolivia, Malta and Peru. It has certainly set down roots in such unlikely habitats as China, England and West Germany, as well as being the most sought-after grape variety in the world's newer wine regions. This is largely because Chardonnay, when planted on the most hallowed ground in Burgundy's heartland, the Côte d'Or, produces such sublimely awe-inspiring wines. And here one is nodding deferentially towards Corton-Charlemange country in the north, but dreaming chiefly of those wines blessed with the word Montrachet, however prefixed or suffixed, in their name. The wines share the opulence of the finer Chardonnays of California, Oregon and Australia, but even a good Puligny-Montrachet and certainly any Chevalier-Montrachet will have discernibly more refinement, more restraint, more rigour, an additional tautness which is the result of — a real understanding of the role of oak? the cooler climate? centuries of tradition? Who knows? But who can fail to fall for it?

Such wines usually come my way by the single bottle: a treat with the first course, or at a formal wine tasting, a pinnacle gained only after addressing the foothills of Pouilly and Pernand-Vergelesses. One day though, at the memorable feast described in Chapter 10 where I was swamped with good things, one of the most sumptuous of them was a clutch of *four* top-quality white burgundies to compare over a dish described on the extraordinary menu as *cassolette de homard aux perles de legumes*. Heaven.

In this context, no less a wine than Leflaive's Chevalier-Montrachet 1982 became — though perhaps only temporarily — a foothill from which to admire André Ramonet's 1979 and 1982 Bienvenue-Bâtard-Montrachets, such was their concentration, attack and sheer class. The Chevalier shared that almost painful purity of top-quality young white burgundy, but was more weighed down by bulk and, in the autumn of 1986, the worse for it. The fourth of these marvels, all of which left me pinching myself and wondering how I had landed a life with such indulgence on the menu, was a slightly toastier and more obvious 1979 Bâtard-Montrachet from Bachelet-Ramonet (whose wines are also sold under the name of Jean-Claude Bachelet, while those of André Ramonet sometimes go under the name Ramonet-Prudhon, each being quite independent of Claude Ramonet who is also based in the village of Chassagne-Montrachet). Burgundy is a complicated place.

I thought about how far the circumstances of these wines' consumption were from those of their production. Here at this unique banquet we were waited on hand and hand by the uniformed staffs of Château d'Yquem, a top restaurant in Bordeaux and another in Mülheim. The wines came in sheerest, long-stemmed Austrian crystal and with them we were served, in delicate flower-strewn china pots, a *beurre blanc* studded with and flavoured by sweet chunks of baby lobster and punctuated with what were verging on bonsai vegetables.

This time, in welcome contrast to the *foie gras* experience, the sweetness of the food was not accentuated, but contrasted with these bone-dry wines, whose steely acidity came as welcome relief from the richness of the dish. The temperature of the white burgundies (not a *vin de table* chill, but definitely cold) was a factor in their refreshment value too.

This and the previous chapter may seem wickedly self-indulgent, and of practical value only to those who regularly

serve lobster and *foie gras* (Concorde's caterers?). I would submit the following more widely applicable principle from this chapter however: that a white burgundy, even at a less exalted level, which is full-bodied as well as being bone dry and relatively high in acid, has the guts to stand up to quite richly sauced fish dishes, yet the finesse to keep the experience an appetizing one.

At another end of the spectrum, a good Mâcon or Pouilly-Fuissé is just the thing for fish pie.

CHAPTER THIRTEEN

INNOCENTS ABROAD
OR WHAT NOT TO DRINK IN A TAVERNA

' "*I rather like bad wine,*" *said Mr Mountchesney;* "*one gets so bored with good wine.*" ' *BENJAMIN DISRAELI,*
SYBIL

In 1977 when I'd been writing about wine for all of two years and reckoned I knew it all, I had a very salutary experience with a restaurant wine list. I'd arrived at Oporto's grand hotel, the Infante de Sagres, in advance of the party I was joining, and the first night I dined alone in its vast and somewhat intimidating dining-room.

I was handed the wine list, studied it carefully, and saw hardly a word I recognized. 'Vinho' and 'verde' leapt off the page as welcome as lifebelts to a man overboard, but the rest might as well have been written in Sanskrit for all that it told me about what was on offer. It came to me in a blinding and uncomfortable flash that this must be how all wine lists look to an awful lot of people. No wonder the wine snob is such a popular hate-figure.

In fact, the best drink on the island, with the exception of the finest sticky, raisiny Commandarias, turned out to be wine lists were only marginally more penetrable. The most expensive bottles carried an impressively ancient vintage and a name such as 'Graves 1962'. For the first few nights we worked our way through these derivatively named survivors.

They were awful. Oxidized and clumsy, they gave us no pleasure. In desperation we tried the cheap bottles and found that, as a general rule, the younger the wine, the fresher, cleaner and unarguably better it tasted. The moral here then is that in a country or region whose wine-making expertise is still struggling for international approval, do not favour antiquity.

In fact, the best drink on the island, with the exception of the finest sticky, raisiny Commandarias, turned out to be something I wouldn't be caught dead drinking back home. The official Cyprus version of the brandy sour consists of a hefty slug of their sweet and naïve domestic brandy, a drop of angostura bitters and some lemon barley water equivalent, extended into a long drink by a generous top-up of soda water. Sounds disgusting, doesn't it? Doubtless it would taste as nasty as it sounds if it weren't drunk in Cyprus's peculiarly golden October sunlight, just as the genuine Russian vodka swigged straight from the bottle would be a dismally viscous experience unless one were striding through the snow up the Nevsky Prospekt at the time. (Why weren't we arrested?) And why is it that a rum-based punch loses its sickly quality under a Caribbean palm tree?

Those who fall in love with a particular wine on holiday are strongly advised to take heed of the above paragraph. Unless the holiday is taken somewhere with conditions very similar to those prevailing back home (Belgium?), beware the apparent metamorphosis undergone by the beloved wine on its journey across the Channel. The voluptuous mouthful can turn into a lean mouthwash; the submissive darling into a snarling monster. True to my nationality, I blame the weather.

If one admits that a wine can be the object of a love affair, then Retsina must be the archetypal holiday romance. Actually it hardly counts as wine to me because its resinated flavour so overwhelms any other more closely associated with the grape. Nonetheless, I must admit that it goes splendidly with basic *taverna* food with its strong seasonings, scent of charcoal, dousings in lemon juice and lashings of oil. Mere geographical association and auto-suggestion probably do not constitute the whole story. Most everyday Greek food and, particularly relevant to British '*tavernas*', Greek-Cypriot food, is fairly crude in texture and strong in flavour. That's why it needs such an unsubtle blockbuster of a wine to wash it down.

CHAPTER FOURTEEN
SATURDAY LUNCH IN LE TOUQUET
BANDOL & SHELLFISH

*'Few pleasures induce a feeling of quite such wickedness as
eating here [La Sorbonne's Casse Croûte]. It is more
expensive than college lunch, more fattening than a yoghurt
and almost always guarantees an afternoon of over-seated
sloth.' AUTHOR AS 'DEBAUCH' IN ISIS, JANUARY 1971*

As anyone who has ever tried to have Saturday lunch at a
good restaurant knows, this is a minority pursuit. At this
time of the week most of the rest of the world is engaged in
virtuously, and often irritably, furnishing their nests rather
than their stomachs. Whether it's a serious commitment to
DIY or the checkout queue, it never seems to be much *fun*.

Perhaps that's why I love Saturday lunch out. There's
nothing like the combination of mild guilt, serious gluttony
and, by the time the first course arrives, the conviction that
what you're doing is infinitely more sensible than putting up
shelves or doing Christmas shopping.

One Saturday lunch was particularly memorable for being
overlaid by the even more poignant emotions associated with
a favourite seaside resort out of season. Le Touquet, or Paris-
Plage as it so ambitiously subtitles itself, has character
dripping from every carefully placed brick. This is Brighton
out of *Fantasia*, the bourgeois seaside villas having been
fashioned in the Twenties and Thirties, presumably to re-
assure their owners that this is a *holiday* by giving them some
fantastical element, whether curved gable, giddy turret or
ambitious vista.

At the end of the town is one of the world's great beaches
— rippled wet, shell-strewn sand up to a mile wide when the
tide's out and all the sky you could wish for. But the town
chooses to turn its back on such a raw (and windy) confron-
tation with nature, and concentrates instead on a criss-cross
of little streets packed with *boutiques de couture, chocolatiers*
and well-cosseted *salons de thé*. In fact, the really smart set
may never have seen the sea at all, for they chose to build
their villas within easy reach of the casino among the pines
and birches which encircle the town. This to Le Touquet is
'la Forêt'.

Flavio Club de la Forêt, easily Le Touquet's grandest gastronomic monument, is in the thick of all this precious, if

45

faded, raciness. Just over the road is the Hotel Westminster, which must have reassured many an English visitor recovering from a choppy cross-Channel flight in the *aéroport*'s heyday. The club is still run, or at least overseen, by the courtly Flavio himself, plus chocoholic dog. (He tried running a place on the Riviera, but it was too hot.)

We went on a beautiful November Saturday when the leaves in the *Forêt* shone gold and the only other customers were a couple from Canada, somewhat glum that we could bring our children to Le Touquet but they couldn't bring their dog.

On the wine list Domaine Ott's red Bandol, Château de Selle 1981 was 170 francs, which in the context of a French Michelin-starred restaurant qualifies for a 'mere'. It seemed enough of a bargain to choose even though our lunch, conventionally, cried out for white. This seemed set to be a meal to break all wine conventions, however, for the young sommelier was quite determined to serve the wine chilled. It was, he told us firmly, *comme il faut*. A compromise was reached whereby we persuaded him to take the bottle out of the ice bucket so that it was the temperature of Beaujolais straight from the cellar rather than that of Sancerre straight from the freezer. Doubtless the Bandol's dependence on the sweetly fruity Grenache grape helped it cope with this apparently Spartan treatment. The low temperature emphasized what acidity the Bandol had, and the tannin was low enough to take the accentuation that always results from a spell in the ice bucket.

Its earthy note was perfect with my succulent *foie gras de haut pays sauternais*, the sweet, molten pink flesh answered by an artfully arranged *gelée* flavoured and coloured by the notorious pink peppercorn. What was more surprising, however, was how delicious the Bandol was with the three other dishes we ordered, each of them shellfish based. Its own inherent sweetness echoed that of the giant orange *langoustine* commas punctuating a sheet of light *beurre blanc*. The low temperature, I have to admit, kept the mixture refreshing. A richer, distinctly spicy *beurre blanc* laced the seafood *marmite*. In this combination the *texture* of each component seemed ideally matched. But the Bandol even managed to flatter the scallops with shoelace strips of spinach in a creamy-lemony sauce. By this time the wine was mellow enough to soften the sharp edges of the *coquilles* dish, but I suspect that, had it been any warmer, it would have seemed too

46

full-bodied. Top marks therefore, if grudgingly awarded, to our sommelier.

The post-prandial glow reached fever pitch as Flavio plied the under-fives with chocolate-dipped twists of orange peel. It was to be a perfect afternoon for a windblown trawl along the beach in brilliant sunlight which stung our eyes and rattled the battened-down shutters on the deserted seaside Dunroamins. And, because it was Saturday rather than the Sunday conventionally laid aside for such diversions, we had the beach to ourselves.

What this experience reaffirmed for me was my long-held belief in many sorts of red wine with many sorts of fish. What it eloquently demonstrated, however, was that there are circumstances in which some reds can unexpectedly benefit from chilling, i.e. those which are a little low in acid, not too high in tannin and which you want to enjoy with something light and delicate, such as shellfish. In other words, to turn a warm-region red into a rosé, chill it. And, of course, to get a restaurant to yourself, have Saturday lunch there.

CHAPTER FIFTEEN

CLARET AND LAMB
THE DIVINE COMBINATION

'It might be worth while binning away a few dozens of the '29s, among them Latour, Margaux and Mouton-Rothschild, and sample a bottle of each annually on one of the many fine days usual in May or June, with a nice little saddle of lamb, or mutton, a Camembert cheese and a couple of friends . . .' IAN MAXWELL CAMPBELL, WAYWARD TENDRILS OF THE VINE

Thus wrote Ian Maxwell Campbell in 1947 in his wonderfully named collection of wine *pensées*. To him, as to generations of similarly experienced gourmets before him, the sheep was the natural supplier of claret fodder, as Bertie Wooster might have put it. Forty years later, Professor Jacques Puisais in *Le Goût Juste* is still recommending as the natural accompaniment to a good Pauillac *'le classique carré d'agneau rôti entouré de cèpes'*. Indeed the salt-marsh sheep raised on the grazing land by the Gironde estuary (too wet for vines) is sometimes called *agneau de Pauillac*, and has been an edible Médoc speciality for decades.

A simple roast of lamb, with garlic and rosemary used extremely sparingly, is the natural choice of main course for a claret lover's dinner, especially if the main course wine(s) come from the left bank of the Gironde — smart stuff from the Médoc or Graves districts. There is good reason for this, though I know that when I was much more of a foodophile, not to say foodomane, than a wine connoisseur, I used to think there was something the faintest bit boring about a plain roast, however good. That, I now see, is the whole point. When the wine is top quality but very subtle and, to use an overworked wine descriptor, complex, it makes sense not to trump what's in the glass with what's on the plate.

It is important to spell things out here, as there are so many interpretations of the red Bordeaux with lamb formula. What I'm talking about is really fine wine, red Bordeaux with a few years in bottle behind it and probably the word *cru* on the label, whether *classé* in the famous 1855 league table of the top sixty-odd châteaux in the Médoc, or its Graves successor in 1959, or perhaps from the junior team of *crus bourgeois*.

A lesser claret — and there are so many of them that are just as delicious in their own way, even if less subtle — can be just the right foil for a lamb dish with more and stronger flavours in it: a garlicky *gigot de sept heures*, a colourful *navarin* or fiercely grilled chops. The direct fruitiness of a young claret provides a backdrop for the food in the same way that the plain roast does for a more complicated wine.

Of course, there is nothing crucial about this blessed roast. No thunderbolt from on high smites those who serve roast beef with fine claret, or indeed those who eat hamburgers with their Lafite. But it may well be the natural slight sweetness of lamb and its particularly succulent texture that is such a flattering partner to wine as relatively dry and austere as the best of Médoc and Graves. I have noticed that St Emilions and Pomerols, with their much greater apparent sweetness, seem particularly happy with the more savoury complement of beef — served fairly plain, of course.

This sort of restriction is tough on creative cooks who are married to great connoisseurs wary of departing from tradition for fear that a drop of balsamic vinegar or strip of lemongrass may interfere with the bouquet of their '61s. Such problems.

Postscript: In the great châteaux where these wonderful wines are produced, the cuisine is kept deliberately simple. The three greatest shocks I had on my first visit to the Médoc were firstly, how blatantly unscenic and indifferent the area was to the tourist, secondly, that this, the greatest wine region on earth, has virtually no indigenous cheese, and thirdly, the local custom of pouring claret over strawberries to eat at the end of the meal. It is true that a drop of lemon juice can make strawberries taste much fruitier, so presumably the acidity in the wine does the same. But the tannin? It seems rather a waste of good claret to me.

CHAPTER SIXTEEN
WHITE WINE AND VENISON
VENISON & VENDANGE TARDIVE
'Gourmandism, when it is shared, has the most marked influence on the happiness which may be found in the married state.' BRILLAT-SAVARIN, LA PHYSIOLOGIE DU GOUT

The wedding was lovely. The honeymoon, true to stereotype, started less than propitiously. The airline left our luggage in Paris. The hire car was nowhere to be seen at Colmar. And our mountain hideaway, a hotel in whose restaurant we expected to ensconce ourselves most evenings, turned out to have lost its chef and entire kitchen staff two weeks before.

Alsace, with its medieval villages huddled up against the pine forests of the Vosges, seemed a romantic, and gastronomically sensible, choice for a late October *lune de miel*. (Extraordinary that the French should use this literal translation of seventeenth-century English.) Our big treat was to be Saturday night dinner at L'Auberge de l'Ill, the famous and long-anticipated three-star inn by the fast-flowing river Ill at Illhaeusern. This was disappointment number four — by no means the fault of the restaurant, but of a temporary and ill-timed *crise de foie* in the newly formed Lander family, exacerbated by the pipe smoke of a nearby German diner. Ah, me — though I can still remember the rich balm of a creamy-green *soupe de grenouilles* before the pipe was lit.

Our compensation for these (minor) blemishes on a wonderful, and certainly memorable, holiday came on Monday. Anyone who is lucky in their job finds it difficult to draw a line between work and play. In my line of business this is nearly impossible, and even on honeymoon a morning's 'work' seemed quite an attractive idea to both Mr and Mrs Lander. We had accordingly arranged a morning session *chez* Hugel, in the cellars on the cobbled main street of Riquewihr where the family has made wine casks or wine for nearly 350 years. Only the clothes and transportation have changed.

Like any 'winery visit', as they are now labelled in commercially astute California, this one involved a chilly, damp tramp around the cellars, during which one learnt a little, working up a thirst for the much more comfortable tasting, during which one learnt a lot. The bread and butter before the cake, so to speak. Except that in this privileged instance Johnny Hugel, the human dynamo in charge of presenting Hugel wines to the world, proposed something rather better than cake: lunch, at L'Auberge de l'Ill.

Well, we would be charmed, we were sure. What luck! A chance to replace Saturday's slightly dismal memory with one enhanced by the presence of such a friend of the family who have run the Auberge for decades. The Hugels and the Haeberlins have grown up together. L'Auberge de l'Ill is Johnny's local, and all this showed during our meal there in the most agreeable way.

There is something about the typical three-star restaurant

that makes it relatively difficult for the newcomer to relax there. This may be partly because the customer is worried: on the one hand about coming up to scratch as a three-star customer, and on the other about whether he is really going to get his money's worth for three-star prices. But at some particularly ambitious French establishments the fault is also on the other side. Some chefs and, particularly, their wives seem to go out of their way to impress upon the customer that he is worshipping at a temple of gastronomy and that he is expected to behave with due reverence. The very napery, as I believe it must be called in such places, seems to exude disapproval.

The Haeberlins and their staff are unusually warm and welcoming to all their customers, but there is no substitute for being guests of one of their best friends. We had a simply glorious meal and, of course, drank far better than we would have done had we been choosing, and paying for, the wine.

Johnny Hugel has a didactic streak in him which, selling such underrated wines as those of Alsace, he needs. Being a natural schoolgirl, I like didacticism and have received few lessons as delicious as the one Johnny Hugel arranged for our main course. His aim was to demonstrate that the white and often deceptively flowery wines of Alsace can be drunk with even very substantial meat dishes. He chose pungently gamey but miraculously tender noisettes of venison in a rich creamy sauce the colour of cocoa. With it he 'proposed', in the polite way of the French language — and who were we to argue? — his Vendange Tardive Tokay d'Alsace 1976.

Alsace wines are characterized by their Germanic grape varieties, well ripened thanks to the Vosges, and fermented to heady, perfumed dryness in which state they remain — in complete contrast to their counterparts, *'Outre-Rhin'*. This was a very special bottle though. It was certainly heady and perfumed, made from the grape known as Pinot Gris in France and Ruländer in Germany, but it had even more substance than most Alsace wines because of its extra ripening weeks on the vine, making its *vendange* (harvest) so *tardive* (late). Hugel have pioneered these strong and rather sweet wines by segregating and separately vinifying the ripest grapes from their most sheltered spots in the sunniest years, such as 1976.

So here we were, eating one of the most strongly-flavoured meat dishes I have had in my life with white wine in which lurked a discernible amount of residual sugar. Not,

on the face of it, a particularly promising marriage, but in fact it was yummy — or rather, as Johnny pointed out, the wine had so much extract (and alcohol) that it was well capable of taking on both meat and sauce in a way that Pinot Noir would have found difficult. The great majority of modern red burgundies with their lighter weight would probably have been reduced to thin ink by the dish. La Tâche might have carried it off, the average Santenay not.

It was an illuminating illustration of how poor a guide to food and wine matching colour makes. And the slight sweetness causes no problems at all provided the wine has enough acidity — just as a sweet Vouvray Moelleux, preferably one whose acidity and perceived sweetness have been dimmed somewhat by age, seems perfection with a fairly richly sauced fish.

There was only one small hitch in this glorious experience. When we arrived at the restaurant, in recognition of the Hugel-Haeberlin alliance, all the front-of-house staff were smartly lined up to be introduced to us honoured guests. Johnny hadn't asked us if we'd been before, and we jolly well weren't going to risk retraction of the invitation by telling him. We couldn't believe the professionalism of the staff as, one by one, they bowed, gravely or respectfully according to rank, but never a one departing by a wink from the ritual of a first-time introduction. This continued until we got to the last in line, the junior sommelier, who blurted out, '*Mais, vous étiez ici samedi soir, n'est-ce-pas?*'

As the rest of the staff looked daggers at him, Johnny wheeled round to us knitting his thick eyebrows, reminding us just how much competition there is between the more important wine families of the region. 'Who brought you here?' he asked sharply, his eyes narrowing. 'Trimbach?'

It also brought home to us that, thanks to the inordinate generosity of the wine trade, the wine writer as paying customer is a phenomenon rarely considered.

CHAPTER SEVENTEEN

WEATHER AND WINE
HOT WEATHER WINES:
'If you desire good wines, these five things are praised in them: Strength, beauty, and fragrance, coolness and freshness.' FALERNO, REGIMEN OF HEALTH

Much has been written, specially by me I feel, about wine and temperature, about the quite major changes in how a wine tastes which can result from serving a wine slightly cooler or a little bit warmer. Just as important though, is the temperature of the taster, or rather the prevailing weather conditions.

I have noticed that I feel like drinking quite different styles of wine in the very varied weather enjoyed by or inflicted on us Britons. One of the few blessings of really cold weather to me is that it gives me an excuse and a will to plunder the bottles in my cellar that seem just too much, too heady in the summer. The intoxicatingly spicy wines of Châteauneuf-du-Pape, sweet fortified wines such as Malaga and Malmsey take on a new charm when the teeth are chattering, and I can even pluck up the courage to unleash vintage port on to my delicate little cranium when there's a snowdrift outside.

In really hot weather, however – such as that enjoyed for months on end in Châteauneuf, Malaga, Malmsey and port country as a curious matter of fact – even much less flamboyant wines can seem inappropriate and ill at ease. Those who organize claret tastings try to avoid midsummer. I remember a dinner held on a sticky London evening at which the principal wine, a Léoville-Barton 1980 chosen by Hugh Johnson in a sensible attempt to stem condemnation of this vintage, might just as well have been served mulled for all the allure it had. And when we went to Guadeloupe one February on what my mother called, with uncharacteristic acerbity, our *third* honeymoon, I remember going off all red wine completely, apart from well-chilled Beaujolais (Georges Duboeuf seemed to have the monopoly) and Chinon. The world's light-bodied, low-tannin reds (see Chapters 7, 8 and 9) come into their own yet again.

This is not just whimsy, and there is more to it than simply seizing upon a chilled drink in preference to one that is not kept in an ice bucket in hot weather. By its nature, wine is a volatile substance, and what we call tasting is sensing the vapour that it gives off. The warmer a wine, or food, the more vapour it gives off and the more of its flavour we can taste. (Compare the smell of a cold and baked apple.) Wine is different, however, in that it contains alcohol which, at a critical point around 65°F, starts to give off its own rather unpleasant fume, 'covering' the much subtler flavour of the wine and making the wine unstable. It doesn't take very long for a glass of wine to reach this temperature in hot weather, which is why it needs the bonus of being pretty cool before it is poured. And one wouldn't want to chill a tannic red wine for fear of making it taste like ink.

There is also the question of drinking wine out of doors. Sometimes it works. I have had several memorable bottles of German wine — '71 Mosel seems to ring a particularly resonant bell — in English gardens. And I will never forget the Tyrrell's Vat 47 Chardonnay savoured afloat off Fremantle (a.k.a. 'Free-o'), with sweet little shellfish plucked from the Indian Ocean by the more energetic members of the crew. But fine red wines drunk in good weather out of doors never seem quite so fine as when their vapour is trapped in a room somewhere.

CHAPTER EIGHTEEN

BRAVING BEIRUT
RAW LIVER & DANGER

*'By using the crudest forms of terror against journalists work-
ing in Lebanon — threats of death, attempted killings, and
actual murder — the Syrian government has just about suc-
ceeded in drawing a damask curtain around its increasingly
perilous condition.'* THE ECONOMIST, AUGUST 2ND 1980

Despite the somewhat swashbuckling title of this book, I've
only ever had one real adventure in the course of my gastronomic travels — one that's endangered my body from without
rather than within, that is. It was the direct result of
accepting an invitation to view at close quarters the Lebanese
answer to Hermitage and Pauillac rolled into one, Château
Musar.

People who live in the world's troublespots seem to believe that they are in no danger at all, until they're blown up
or door-stepped themselves. Each new day's survival is
taken as vindication of this view. So it was that the engaging
Serge Hochar, surely the world's most determined wine producer, invited myself and Tony Lord, of *Decanter* magazine,
to Beirut in September 1980. We must have been mad to go,
though I see that I chose a notebook with a black cover to
record the visit.

First there was the visa, a stamp of cedar issued in a seedy
little London mews. Then the MEA plane on which only the
first five rows offered any protection from the haze of pungent smoke which hung over the rest of the cabin. At the airport there were machine-guns everywhere but no sign of
Serge. A Lebanese-born Catholic had, as early as 1980, to
send an envoy called Mahmoud to escort his guests through
the dozen checkpoints between the airport and his apartment
in the Christian sector.

We passed the refugee encampments, already well estab-
lished, and then in the main body of the city I was astonished
to see no obvious vestige of the smart hotels I remembered
from my previous visit in 1970. What remained of Beirut's
many modern blocks had also been shelled, visibly wrench-
ing whole sections of the buildings out of their sockets and on
to the wasteland below. Almost all apartment blocks were by
now pockmarked with snipers' bullets.

Most of the cars were equally battered remnants of

Beirut's more prosperous recent past: bullet-holed, low-slung Mercedes, even the odd Jaguar. But Beirut was still founded on commerce. By the side of the road, just next to the sandbags, were piles of bulbous watermelons, the stalagmites of commercial life, with their stalactite counterparts, bunches of loofas, hanging from countless dusty awnings. Once into the Christian sector, the roadside shrines twinkled, as immaculately kept as conceived, while *American Gigolo* played at the main cinema.

The Hochar apartment was on the fourth floor above the *chocolatier de luxe* where he continued to ply his Godiva concession. I think he probably owned the whole block. We sat on the balcony watching the sun set over the debris, drinking coffee. The wife of the best wine maker between Florence and Fremantle does not drink.

We were to be kept, tantalizingly, from Serge Hochar's wonderful wine that evening too, at the most adventurous meal I've ever had. We drove north — checked by more teenage soldiers — into the hills, past pine trees swaying in the moonlight, to the Mounir restaurant at Broumana. Here was *le tout* Beirut — the Hochars had to stoop and embrace each gilded, glamorous and vital party — and it was possible to forget the troubles, until the next power cut plunged everything into eerily silent darkness.

As they kissed and gossiped (in French) with the Lebanese they'd grown up with, we eyed the spanking clean marble counter with its neat little silver trays piled high with careful arrangements of the local delicacies. This could almost be a Marylebone High Street *pâtissier*, except that these were no sweetmeats. This, *the* smart summer restaurant, was clearly an offal joint. There were roses re-created with carved slices of raw liver, fortresses of skewered meats, neat little mounds of what Serge airily referred to as 'sheep's hearts, balls and rates' (rates?), and lots more in that line.

I'm not a conservative eater — the black notebook had, I think, been given to me by a Macedonian host who had served a sheep's head earlier that summer — but all those checkpoints had left their mark on my stomach. I was starting to feel just a little queasy.

'Our first dinner,' announced Serge as we sat down, 'is to be an arak dinner. Wine is fine with Lebanese cooking, but arak is better with Lebanese *food*.' I began to see what he meant. Throughout a long and extremely filling evening, there was disturbingly little evidence of the restaurant's employing a chef. Veg prep, yes. Chopping and puréeing definitely a speciality. (In fact, just about everything we were served seemed to prove one theory I'd heard about Lebanese food — that its intricate preparation kept the wife too busy in the kitchen to complain about her secluded lifestyle.) But actual cooking was thin on the plate. This was food — meat and veg — in the raw. Perhaps it had something to do with the frequent blackouts, but I doubt it.

The meal was notable not only for its inherent *crudité*, but also for its copiousness. Today, if ever I'm served in some Camden Town taverna something they call *meze*, I smile. There are seventeen things listed in my black notebook until they peter out into the feeble note, 'And many more dishes'. Each table had been issued with what appeared to be a small compost heap of greenery — edible, of course. Then came pistachios fresh from the tree, looking like tatty little radishes in their scarlet skins. There was also *hummus* and, of course, *baba ghanoush*, the smoky aubergine cream to spoil Camden Town for us forever; crumbly white goat's cheese; a mould of cheese and thyme; stuffed vine leaves; spicy little rissoles and small meat parcels; garlic cream; a flat cake of thin pastry sandwiched with meat and pine nuts; fried cheese-filled *filo; kibbeh*, pink ovals of raw ground meat with cracked wheat; little mounds of yoghurt; an almost neurotically chopped salad of green leaves called *roka*; wafers of *basterma*, raw meat hung and smoked; a local blue cheese remarkably like a Roquefort; salads galore; *batarekh*, slices of compressed fish eggs and, obviously the *pièce de résistance* — a wooden board on which was a pile of brown peppers, mint, green peppers and tomatoes as big as grapefruit trying to distract us from a line of raw fillet, one of raw fat and another of raw liver. 'All lamb,' Serge smiled and nodded encouragingly. 'Delicious.' He picked up a particularly pink and slithery slice of the liver and then moved it ceremoniously and incontrovertibly towards my lips.

What does one do in these circumstances? *Rosemary's Baby* had not convinced me that this was the right way to eat liver. Yet clearly this was an important symbolic gesture. To refuse would have been to make a deeply ungracious statement. I ate it, of course, and then blessed Serge for his wisdom in choice of lubrication. The Lebanese answer to ouzo and raki quickly washed away the traces of this titbit, just the wrong side for me of the boundary patrolled by steak tartare between the edible and the inedibly raw. Even a wine as

powerful as Château Musar, whose 1970 and 1959 claretish heavyweights must rank among the greats of the wine world, could not have done the job half as well.

We moved from one glass of arak to the next, always by tradition in a new glass, and Serge told us how his family started to distil arak only five years ago, when they were holed up in the winery to the north of Beirut 'during wartime' and set to distillation as a way of disposing of some of their older, less satisfactory wines.

As the lights flickered and died once more I started to feel that we too might find ourselves holed up by the exigencies of war with nothing but a few thousand bottles of Château Musar and some raw meat for company.

We had a fascinating few days, and got quite used to the sight of worry beads and guns, even to the Israeli jets patrolling high above the Bekaa Valley where Serge's grapes were grown, and harvested by non-drinking Bedouin tribeswomen. However, I was only too pleased to hand over the money demanded with menaces at that angst-ridden airport from all those who wished to leave it.

CHAPTER NINETEEN
WHITE WINES FIT FOR A STEAK
SEX AND WINE
'Oh some are fond of Spanish wine, and some are fond of French,
And some'll swallow tay and stuff fit only for a
wench.' JOHN MASEFIELD, CAPTAIN STRATTON'S FANCY

There is a popular theory, held almost exclusively by men, that certain wines are 'women's wines', and that others, generally rather superior ones, can be truly appreciated only by the male of the species.

Where I was brought up, in the rural Cumbria of the Fifties and Sixties, meals out were judged on the basis of how many courses were provided per pound sterling, no matter if one of these courses was half a hard-boiled egg smothered in what was then called salad cream and another was a small pudding bowl of packet soup. Where these cafés and dining-rooms of hotels, motels and 'country clubs' were licensed, the women of the party would be issued with a suitable ration of lurid yellow liquid labelled Sauternes to drink with their steak, while the chaps looked for something interesting and red.

Now it is true that many women, during pregnancy, find red wine suddenly and unaccountably unpalatable, but I don't see that as sufficient justification for positing that women have different tastes and preferences in wine throughout their lives. Women's alcohol absorption mechanisms may not be as efficient as men's, but our tasting equipment is identical.

It is natural for the nascent wine drinker of either sex to be weaned on slightly sweet wines, as witness the high residual sugar level in the red and white versions of such novitiate brands as Piat d'Or. But unless the prevailing social climate insists that they stick with the sweet, more experienced drinkers soon begin to appreciate rather drier stuff. (And many eventually graduate to the really sophisticated wine drinker's view that there is a place for wines of all levels of sweetness, even Sauternes.)

It does seem, however, that in very general terms more women than men prefer white to red wine and vice versa. The reasons in this case, too, probably have more to do with conditioning than physiology. Some postgraduate student may wish to expand and expound on this hypothesis, providing socio-psycho explanations for it, perhaps even breast-beating denunciations of it, but this is not the place. All I wish to point out is that those of either sex who much prefer white wine to red, or have the relatively common bad reaction to the higher histamine content of red wines, should not feel remotely uneasy about drinking white wine with meat.

For the reasons outlined in Chapter 9, 'Red Wines with Fish', the white wine with fish rule is no more than a rusty convention. And as hinted at in Chapter 16, 'White Wine and Venison', there is a wide range of whites that are just as delicious with even quite sturdy meat dishes as many reds. Again, 'weight' of the wine is the crucial factor. Provided the white wine is not too light, i.e. short of alcohol and body, and its strength of flavour is well matched to that of the food, then the combination can be sublime.

The wines of Alsace are obvious candidates, though I had assumed that it was only because the Tokay d'Alsace is the least florally aromatic of the Alsace grape varieties that it was so winning with venison on the visit to L'Auberge de l'Ill already described. Much more recently however, I tried a Gewurztraminer Vendange Tardive 1964 from Preiss Zimmer with a salad of strongly flavoured duck meat slivers salted and crisped under a salamander, together with some

warm waxy potatoes and seaweed-like shavings of black truffles. Admittedly, the usually overpowering intensity of Gewurztraminer perfume had been muted a bit by the two decades in bottle; the wine was off dry rather than sweet, and could not have been richer and heavier — a Sumo champion of a white wine. It grappled most appetizingly with this strongly flavoured salad, and happily took on another salty dish, freshly salted cod with *purée* and garlic on a dark *jus*, afterwards. The slight sweetness of these super-ripe grapes undoubtedly helped.

A less rarefied combination, however, is any moderately forceful dry white with a meat dish, the better and more nuanced the wine, the simpler the food. Any straightforward grilled meat, for instance, can be a fine foil for a really interesting white burgundy, white Rhône or Chardonnay or Semillon from any of the world's not-too-chilly wine-growing regions — particularly one that is sufficiently old to have developed some discernibly different layers of flavour.

Such wines can also hit the spot with creamily-sauced meats, and even the lighter meats in general. A vibrant California Chardonnay in the Edna Valley mould was a delight with the slight sweetness of sweetbreads and morels in a light cream sauce enlivened with tarragon.

If the meat is dressed in soy, or indeed any other sauce or marinade which reacts adversely with tannin, then a white wine is actually much better than a red.

I do reckon there are certain white wines which are just too light to stand up to a strong savoury flavour, or indeed any food at all. Aromatic whites made far from the equator, such as New Zealand Muller-Thurgaus, lightly chaptalized English and Luxembourg Elblings fall into this category, as do Germany's lighter wines, whose naturally low alcoholic strength has been diluted by the unfermented grape juice — the *Sussreserve* commonly used to sweeten Germany's more ordinary wines. The new German Trocken and Halbtrocken (dry and half dry) wines with their average alcohol level of more than 10 per cent are more obvious candidates for the dining table.

Here conditioning starts to play its irresistible, though not necessarily logical, part once more. A scent — say, typically, the almost honeyed, floral perfume of a Rheingau Riesling — which has for years been associated with sweet wines seems downright odd with savoury dishes. Though it must be said that no one could be working harder to counteract this somewhat blimpish reaction than the top Rheingau producers themselves.

Vive les blancs! Though remember that most whites up to the job of accompanying a main course will have sufficient extract that they shouldn't be left in the fridge or ice bucket too long.

CHAPTER TWENTY

GOOD, PLAIN FOOD

WHAT WE REALLY EAT

'[Wine] awakens and refreshes the lurking passions of the mind, as varnish does the colours which are sunk in a picture, and brings them out in all their natural glowings.' ALEXANDER POPE

So far, you might be forgiven for thinking that my diet was one long succession of dishes *de luxe*: a *langouste* here, a slice of *foie gras* there, not *another* three-star restaurant this evening.

My life is not like that actually — nor, I suspect, is yours. In fact, thanks to the work of Mr John Squire Kirkham of the London Clinic on my loved one's stomach, the food I eat at home is probably considerably plainer, and certainly more meat-dominated, than the national average.

I reckon I'm pretty well qualified therefore to recommend wines to go with such staples as sausages and shepherd's pie. In our household we drink wine every night, and see no contradiction, only elevation, in matching exotic foreign liquids with stolid domestic solids. I must admit though, that in a more temperate or economical household, a glass of water or even a cup of tea would go really rather well with many British basics.

It is difficult to make blanket recommendations since these basics vary so much in flavour and intensity, but here are a few of the distinctly less adventurous main dishes (some distinctly un-British) served *chez* Lander with wines we've found to be particularly successful.

Bacon: Is it because I know they're 'difficult' with wine that I've convinced myself I don't like fried eggs? (See next chapter.) Anyway, I can strongly recommend bacon as a good excuse for drinking one of the many slightly sweet-tasting young light- to medium-bodied reds that are made in California, Australia and Spain. It's the familiar sweet and salt principle that makes this combination work, but the wines need to be frank and fruity, as opposed to complex and mature, to meet something as humble as bacon on its own ground.

Beef Stroganoff: I like the formulation of spices and seasonings prescribed by the *Silver Palate Cookbook* — lots of everything from Hungarian paprika thru', as they would doubtless say, Dijon mustard to Worcestershire sauce. This means that only a fairly fiery wine need apply for the post of glass-filling with my Stroganoff. I find southern Rhône reds, such as Châteauneuf-du-Pape, Gigondas, Vacqueyras and top quality Côtes-du-Rhône of the Château de Fonsalette sort do the job extremely well thanks to their similar make-up of different flavours and considerable weight through sheer force of alcohol level. The purist in me searches in vain for a really robust red exported from Hungary, but Bulgaria (not the same thing at all, I do realize) can certainly oblige — notably with the powerful indigenous grapes Mavrud and, even more concentrated, Melnik.

Calves' liver: This popular source of protein and iron, so much more satisfying cut thicker than the restaurant norm, tastes notably sweet for a meat. As with its relative, *foie gras*, it is easy to make a sickly combination by drinking too sweet a wine with it. For that reason calves' liver is best with a very dry and perhaps fairly tannic red wine or, ideally, a substantial white wine with lots of acidity. Good quality Loire whites made from the Chenin Blanc grape, such as Vouvray,

Bonnezeaux or Coteaux du Layon can be delicious, particularly if, in the case of the sweeter *moelleux* or *demi-sec* examples, age has dimmed their apparent sweetness. (This is the sort of under-appreciated and under-valued wine, incidentally, that is also divine with many fish dishes. Its acidity provides the perfect cutting edge for the richness of a *beurre blanc*.)

Pasta: When in doubt, boil a cauldron of water. This is a habitual prelude to the sort of meal to delight not just the (barely distinguishable) senses of taste and smell, but the tactile sense as well. A good part of the pleasure of pasta is coping with its different shapes and observing how each accommodates the different sauces. These tend to determine the sort of wine that goes best, but if ever a single wine style were made for pasta of all sorts, even *carbonara*, it is that described in Chapter 7. A pasta dressed in a creamy sauce of smoked salmon slivers, however (pasta as Manhattan rather than *Mezzogiorno* phenomenon), might call for some dramatic tinkering with the formula. This may even be the moment for Piedmont's full but gorgeously aromatic white Arneis. The acidity of *pesto* seems more at home with a white too, though ideally one a little earthier than Arneis, such as a wine based on Vernaccia, Greco, Grechetto or even Semillon.

Roast chicken: It is near-impossible to enjoy basic chickens nowadays. To experience anything like the flavour of chicken, as opposed to the pong of fish meal, it is usually necessary to spend a bit extra on a corn-fed fowl or the gamier, and fleshier *poulet noir*. We find that a roasted specimen of either kind is delightfully therapeutic after too much rich food, though it is tempting to enrich the chicken by dousing it in sherry vinegar and slipping a creamy cheese or some butter and fresh green herbs between skin and flesh. This is the dish with which to wheel out a good, self-confident rosé, such as that from Mas de Daumas Gassac in the Hérault, Val Joanis' from the Lubéron, the Tuscan Rosa di Sanpolo, or one of Navarra's best with masses of flavour and a refreshingly low temperature, no matter how *démodé* chicken and rosé may sound.

Risotto: A major part of the joy of a roast chicken is that it provides the basis of a risotto, with the nut-hard arborio rice whose every grain survives intact the reduction of chicken stock and some white wine. Risotto of most sorts, and certainly the chicken with mushroom or walnut risotto prevalent in my household, is a relatively gentle, subtle dish which can easily be overwhelmed by too powerful a wine. Drinking the wine used in cooking makes sense, and this is one of the few savoury dishes that I find sit quite happily next to a glass of Germanic wine, a good sturdy Kabinett from the Rheinpfalz, for instance, or a spicy young Grüner Veltliner or Gumpoldskirchner from Australia (though these are thin on the selves at the moment).

Sausages: There are, naturally, sausages and sausages. There's the industrial sort whose production methods seem to hog, if you'll excuse the word, the screen in television programmes about the evils of animal fats. Entrail slurry is apparently a major ingredient. We prefer our entrails chopped and mashed in a more *artisanal* fashion and accordingly stick to sausages bought in expensive delicatessens and grocery shops where people come to speak Italian. The sausages taste better. To convert sausages into a dish that actually calls for wine requires some ingredient to soak up that animal fat: lentils with little *salsiccie*, small white *cannellini* beans with smoked *saucisses d'Auvergne*, warm potato salad with *bratwurst*. Thus is the fry-up converted into a *dish*, delicious with full-flavoured, rustic wines such as Rioja of Cune or La Rioja Alta quality, and many of Portugal's under-priced reds. Most Cumberland sausage, my own particular regional speciality, is so high in pepper that, like curry, it belongs out of wine-drinking country.

Shepherd's pie: This is a great favourite, much called for (at, on average, five minutes' notice) by the under-fives. They drink apple juice or Ribena, while their parents prefer Beaujolais or the sort of non-grand bordeaux called 'lunchtime claret' by those who expect something better for dinner. Red bordeaux considered suitable for lunchtimes are those either from light vintages, or lesser properties or lesser appellations from recent ones. With so many flavours baked together in the shepherd's pie, there seems a need for a wine that is relatively pure in flavour and has some refreshing acidity. If the shepherd's pie were made of stronger stuff than just the remains of a roast of lamb, however — perhaps spiked and flavoured with tiny cubes of salami — then the might of the southern Rhône would definitely be called for by the wine drinkers of the family.

CHAPTER TWENTY-ONE
PARIAHS OF THE LARDER?
DIFFICULT FOODS FOR WINE

'Our Garrick's a salad; for in him we see oil, vinegar, sugar and saltness agree.' OLIVER GOLDSMITH, RETALIATION

As someone who earns her living tasting wine, I'm often asked whether I have to take special care of my palate. 'Do you have to avoid curries?' people enquire solicitously. Luckily the palate is not nearly such a sensitive little flower as all this concern makes it sound, and since our most sensitive tasting equipment is located at the top of the nose rather than in the mouth, a heavy cold is a much more serious handicap to wine appreciation than a powerful Vindaloo.

In most cases the effects of a mouthful of one thing can be eradicated by rinsing with a mouthful of water, or chewing something absorbent and neutral, such as bread. But there are some foods which have, rightly or wrongly, been regarded as inimical to wine and unfit for the dining table of the true wine-lover: artichokes, asparagus, vinegar, eggs and chocolate join very hotly spiced foods in this category.

I know there are some people who can hardly enjoy even a bowl of cereal, let alone a steak, unless it has been doused in Tabasco or some other hot pepper sauce of almost painful intensity, but I have never been able to see the point. Why anaesthetize the taste-buds so that the efforts of the cook and the flavour of the food itself can't even be sensed? It is true that very hot food simply leaves the tongue and inside of the mouth feeling extremely raw and numb, and in no fit state to enjoy something as subtle as wine. Nor are its ravages confined to the mouth either, as most spices are very aromatic and tend to zoom up the nose to interfere with the tasting equipment there.

All these comments apply only to *really* hot dishes of course. Subtle, well-integrated spices do no damage to the tasting mechanism at all and a considerable, increasing proportion of the food called Indian, and even Mexican, will not overpower a full-bodied wine. Because the food itself is 'hot', however, we usually feel we want a cool drink with it, which means that the full-bodied wine had better be white. Some Alsace wines as robust as, say, Léon Beyer's Gewurztraminers can make a sophisticated lubricant for Indian dishes that can properly be described as *haute cuisine*. Their own relatively aromatic nature helps them stand up to the pungency of the spices.

Globe artichokes present a different, yet quite real problem. As Harold McGee, that invaluable interpreter on the arts/science frontier, explains in his book, *On Food and Cooking*, artichokes contain a substance, dubbed cynarin once it had been isolated, which seriously distorts most people's tasting perceptions. To the great majority of tasters, even water tastes quite different after a mouthful of cynarin. They say it tastes 'sweet'. I think the difference is more subtle than that, but there is no doubt that wine drunk in between mouthfuls of artichoke tastes quite different from how it normally tastes. It seems to me to taste almost metallic. The nose, the most important part of a wine's flavour after all, is unaffected, but a mouthful of the wine is knocked out of shape.

This sensitivity to cynarin varies from person to person and is probably determined genetically. Individual sensitivities to almost any substance, even something as basic as sugar, vary enormously, but what makes the artichoke problem worth writing about is that cynarin-sensitivity affects so high a proportion of the population.

Although I am extremely cynarin-sensitive and a confirmed, not to say addicted, wine drinker, I see this as no reason to eliminate artichokes and their unique sensory pleasures from my diet. After all, they're quite watery themselves, so if nothing is drunk with them, no terrible thirst will ensue. I tend to drink wine before them and after them, taking a good mouthful of water or bread between artichoke and wine. I wouldn't choose to serve artichokes at a meal designed to show off top quality wines, but one should never forget that bread or water can work wonders.

Asparagus seems to me to affect wine in a similar, though less dramatic way, so it is quite conceivable that it contains its own temperance-touting substance which has not yet been isolated. Again, my love for wine is not great enough to deny me the sweet, spring-like pleasure of this vegetable that we English nurture so well.

A lot of fuss has been made of the dire consequences of eating eggs while drinking wine — or is it vice versa? Whichever it is, the fuss is overplayed. Once eggs are properly cooked and integrated into a dish they pose no threat to wine.

Cheese soufflé is a favourite first course among many of France's top wine producers. One of the most glamorous meals I can remember was lunch on the terrace overlooking the wide, sleepy river outside Christian Moueix's house in Libourne. The glamour perhaps owed more to Marie-Laure Moueix, but the cheese soufflé was *impeccable* and certainly a fine partner to the wine in the household whose 'house wine' is Château Pétrus.

The only (small) problem for wine is soft egg yolk, which, like chocolate (examined in detail on page 85), has an inconvenient habit of coating the inside of the mouth and sealing up the taste-buds. Again, this in no way affects the smellable flavour of the wine, and can be countered by a well-chewed mouthful of bread vide *œufs meurette* in Burgundy.

The anti-vinegar camp's argument is different. The theory is that anything too acidic will bring out the worst in a wine, just as something bland, like mild cheese, will do the reverse. Hence the wine trade adage to 'buy on an apple and sell on cheese'. As one who has systematically punctuated sips of a wide range of wines with sips of neat commercial tarragon wine vinegar, I can report that the effect of vinegar on wine is also much exaggerated. The wines stood up remarkably well to this sousing of the taste-buds. This is just as well since acidity in general, and vinegar in particular, have been invading our plates with force of late.

I certainly wouldn't vouch for the usually horribly strong malt vinegar, but any dressing or sauce based on a more subtle vinegar, or on lemon juice, can even enhance some wines. I tried a particularly lean 1984 basic Bordeaux *petit château* wine the other day that tasted considerably plumper and more attractive after my *sushi* vinegar-dressed salad than before. It is, after all, logical that an acid wine will seem less acid after something even more acid, just as a sweet wine seems less sweet (and more acid) after eating a particularly sweet pudding.

The most stylish salad dresser I have ever seen in action is a particularly stylish dresser herself, Margrit Mondavi. She was preparing lunch for the customary dozen or two guests who are entertained daily at the Robert Mondavi Winery in the Napa Valley, interspersing food preparation with the most dashingly casual flower arrangement and a line in baby-dandling that brought a glow of pride to this mother's heart. Just before the meal she bore off to the kitchen a bottle of her husband's flagship wine (Opus One was still at the dandle

70

stage itself then), Robert Mondavi Cabernet Sauvignon Reserve of a particularly mature and toothsome vintage. No cook's perk this but a practical way of solving the 'problem' of serving salad with a top quality wine.

CHAPTER TWENTY-TWO
WINE AND CHEESE
A DANGEROUS LIAISON
'If I had a son who was ready to marry, I would tell him: "Beware of girls who don't like wine, truffles, cheese or music." ' COLETTE

Wine and cheese is such a celebrated combination that it even has a (rather precious) social event named after it. Yet it's a combination that is fraught with physical danger. The right cheese can be a flattering sop to a glass of wine, but the wrong one can destroy it.

In Britain we tend to bracket them together perhaps because our national interest in them as representatives of a more exotic lifestyle began at more or less the same time, towards the end of the Sixties. Perhaps more vividly than any other image, that of *vin rouge* and Brie came to signal the sophisticated side of the borderline between gastronomy and mere refuelling.

It took me some time, therefore, before I objectively ex-amined the wine and cheese proposition. The first thing to be sorted out, of course, is that major question of whether to have cheese before or after the sweet course. This is one of those issues that, like religion, politics and nuclear defence policy, can break up families.

Let us just state then that, on those rare occasions when it can field two whole courses after the main one, ours is a cheese-first household. Classically this is advised so that the main course wine can be 'finished up' with the cheese. In entertaining practice here, however, as happens in most other wine-besotted households of my acquaintance, the cheese often provides an excuse for opening up an even older or grander bottle of red. Then, when the savoury bit of the meal is over, in a single succession of courses, we all move on to a *bonne bouche* at the end. This seems to me more sensible than hopping to and fro between savoury and sweet, but I never cease to be amazed by how many people clearly dis-agree with me. (The most convincing case for sweet-first I ever saw was put up by the *Spectator*'s man at the table, Digby Anderson. After a pudding of some sort, he says he likes to flow seamlessly from cheese into what was originally called dessert, all nutcrackers and odd fruits, calling for dec-anters of dessert wines the while.)

The positioning of the cheese course is a one-off doctrinal decision. The interesting bit is matching different cheeses and wines. My researches were given a considerable fillip in December 1985 when the English Country Cheese Council asked me to write a pamphlet on matching wines with vari-ous English cheeses. A plan was devised whereby Paxton & Whitfield, the smelliest shop in Jermyn Street, would send me each Friday half a pound each of the 13 least obscure native cheeses and I would sample them over the following week with as many different wines as possible. (I suppose if I'd been really quick off the mark, I could have got the Coun-cil to send me a case or two of wine each week too. . .)

Each Friday one box of greaseproof paper and ripened curd would be replaced in the larder by another, to give a great deal of illuminating pleasure to this palate.

I had already noted that, in very general terms, wine is happier with the average English cheese than with the typical *fromage* or *formaggio*. The trouble with the opulent texture of some soft imports, such as Brie, Camembert, Vacherin, Pont-l'Evêque, Epoisses, Maroilles, Munster and even some

72

delicious Reblochon, is that it is so often rather rubbery, easily coating the tongue and immobilizing, or at least disabling, the taste-buds. The problem seems to be particularly acute with cheeses which are ripened from the outside rather than from within, as in the Cheddar recipe.

A further problem in Britain arises from senile Bries and Camemberts which have taken on an ammoniacal note that goes ill with something as delicate as most wines. One of the many great joys of a visit to France is the chance to plunder such well-kept cheeseboards, but I'm careful not to waste a really fine wine on the sorts of cheese listed above. I think it's significant that Bordeaux boasts no great local cheese and that its châteaux' cheeseboards sport mainly the firm cheeses of the Dutch, their traditional trading partners.

Needless to say, after only a week or two of the Paxton & Whitfield regime, much as I love English cheese, I was dying for my French favourites — the gorgeous creaminess of Chaource, the shocking 75 per cent of greasy matter offered by the likes of Explorateur, not to mention my beloved Italians, such as Fontina, Grana and Mascarpone, so that my midwinter of detailed research into the wine and cheese question was not restricted by chauvinism.

By concentrating, and rather greasy note-taking, I was able to learn a great deal, and realized that the four most telling factors in cheese are its texture, its saltiness, its acidity and its strength of flavour. Some of the textures described earlier make the cheese an unsuitable partner for a wine of any notable quality, but fairly hard cheeses — almost all English, many Dutch and Swiss, Cantal and the Parmesan family — can make great partners for very good wine. They may sometimes be crumbly, but they are definitely solid rather than liquid or cream, which means that they are clean-tasting and make no alteration to our basic tasting faculties.

All British cheeses are fairly salty — Cheshire, Caerphilly and Stilton especially so — and they are generally quite acid compared with, say, Gruyère. The saltier the cheese, the 'sweeter' the wine can be and, just as with any other food, it works best to try to match the strength of flavour of the wine with the powerfulness of the cheese. Any cheese will taste more powerful the longer it's been aged, and blue cheeses are in general much more strongly flavoured than the rest.

This means that, for instance, a young, fairly straightforward cheese, such as a White Wensleydale, a young Cheshire

73

either annatto-dyed or not, or what might be called a simple young goat (if such an animal doesn't sound like a contradiction in terms), is best with a fairly light red — 'lunchtime claret'? Beaujolais? — or a white that is relatively assertive either in body, such as a good white burgundy or Tokay d'Alsace, or in sweetness.

There is no earthly reason why the wine served with cheese must be red. The convention is that a meal progresses from white to red, dry to sweet and young to old, but the sweeter whites suitable for cheese could happily take their place in the conventional progression. I remember the unexpected and prolonged thrill of a bottle of Schloss Schönborn Johannisberger Klaus Auslese 1971 sipped with that cheese of limited international *réclame*, Southwold *chèvre*. (Should it or shouldn't it be called 'Southwold goat'? One can so easily understand why it isn't.) Here was an example of the principle underlying the famous port and Stilton: sweet and salt, but in a summer rather than winter version. The sweet Rheingau wine, for all the wonderfully high-toned flowers-and-steel bouquet wrought by its fourteen years of development in bottle, was still fairly light-bodied, and was a perfect match for the refreshing delicacy of the young goat's cheese.

Sancerre and Pouilly Fumé (will someone tell me a foolproof way of distinguishing them blind?) are sometimes suggested as natural partners for the infant precursors of *crottins de chavignol*, little white patties of young local Loire *chèvre*. I've tried and enjoyed this combination at the beginning of a meal, when the cheese is served as part of a carefully dressed salad (a particularly apt use for walnut oil), either *au four* or *au natur*, but I can't see the introduction of a young, tart Loire white towards the end of a meal with the arrival of the cheese course being very successful. Oh, the niceties of the perfect table!

In a sense, cheese works best with dry white wines when it is being eaten — as it so very often is by me — as a meal in its own right, constituting a light lunch or supper as soufflé, rarebit, cheese on toast or, most frequently, in the raw slices, shavings, crumbs and chunks that define it, with good bread.

Sweet wines, whether white or red, can be sublime with cheese — indeed are easier to match successfully than what the Australians call 'dry reds'. They are best with fairly salty, acid, powerfully flavoured cheeses such as the blues, as witness Roquefort and Yquem, the very successful French answer to port and Stilton. Malmsey or Bual madeira, old Cream and sweetened Oloroso sherry, old tawny or vintage port and any full-bodied sweet wine, such as a good Sauternes, can be a delight with blue cheeses, and even with a particularly mature Cheddar. Sugar in the glass and salt on the plate.

I write in the middle of what appears to be a national shortage of farmhouse Cheddar more than about three months old. I have great memories, however, of year-old Cheddars (which, like year-old Goudas, are starting to become problematical partners for wine, so pungent are they), nibbled with a wide range of jewel-textured, fortified wines, as well as with a bizarre Australian one-off from McWilliam's, labelled Private Bin 903 1958 Pedro Sauterne (sic). This, one of Australia's first bottlings of botrytized wine (wine concentrated to ultra-sweetness by the *botrytis cinerea* fungus), was made from Pedro Ximenez grown at their Hanwood vineyard in irrigated New South Wales. It was very sweet and enormously *big*, not unlike some of the McWilliams themselves. A Southwold *chèvre* would have buckled under the impact of this bottle, which I keep to this day, even though it is embossed with the warning 'This Bottle Always Remains the Property of City Bottle Co Pty Ltd Sydney'.

Younger Cheddars are perhaps *the* ideal cheeses for wines, though much of the cheese sold in blocks by that name is worthy only of a fast melt. Good examples have a confident texture, a little bit of salt and a little bit of acid, and are not too powerfully flavoured. A three-month-old Cheddar from the enterprising Chewton Magna, the Waldegrave home farm, was wonderful in November 1986 with wines that, like the cheese, were fine and concentrated but still in the bloom of youth, such as Heitz Martha's Vineyard 1975, the archetypal eucalyptoid California Cabernet Sauvignon, and a notably juicy Beaune, Les Chouachoux 1976 from Machard de Gramont.

Other successful liaisons between English cheese and wine, which I tried and tested in my experimental period, were the saltier young cheeses, such as white Stilton and Caerphilly with 'sweet-tasting' reds, such as those from the southern Rhône and Provence; very robust reds, such as Barolo and Hermitage with a cheese as powerful as a mature Red Leicester; and a full-blooded, hot-country red, such as Zinfandel or Shiraz to obliterate the horribly fake taste of Sage Derby.

One delightful side-effect of the whole business was that each week's consignment (I had to come clean in the the New Year and admit that the main thrust of my researches was over), contained some *plain* Derby, a delicious nutty cheese that was just as well behaved a partner for wine as mild Cheddar and Double Gloucester.

If ever there were a reason for culinary jingoism, it is our (allied) heritage in cheese and connoisseurship. I could live on wine and cheese, though count me out of the eponymous parties.

CHAPTER TWENTY-THREE

ALARM-CLOCK WINE TASTING
THE PERILS OF TOOTHPASTE
'Botticelli isn't a wine, you Juggins! Botticelli's cheese!' *PUNCH 1894*

In 1979 I lived for a while in a flat just behind the Wallace Collection in Manchester Square. It must have been the proximity that made me agree to join a group of wine tasters at Findlater's in Wigmore Street in their early morning training sessions for the Master of Wine examination.

Half the marks for this unique exam, the nearest thing the wine trade has to bar finals, go to papers deemed 'Practical', i.e. assessing and often identifying a dozen mystery wines at a time. Tasting wines 'blind' is basically a sport, one of the few that doubles as dinner party entertainment, and you have to be in condition to perform well, which is why Master of Wine candidates find themselves doing silly things like tasting two dozen wines blind every day for the week before the exams in May.

Throughout the spring we met on Thursday mornings at 8.30, bleary-eyed over the bottles. I suppose I treated it as a breakfast substitute. I lived so close I would set my alarm for eight o'clock and had little time for anything other than the most cursory of *toilettes*. The first couple of times I found it unaccountably difficult to taste the wines in the cellars Findlater's had so kindly put at our disposal. Then I realized why.

Toothpaste. I was brushing my teeth and then immediately trying to taste a high-acid liquid, wine. Things started falling into place. For some time I had noticed that orange juice tasted pretty revolting just after toothpaste, as indeed it still does. Forget artichokes, asparagus, eggs and chocolate. Most toothpastes' combination of strong mint and some sugar is lethal for any fruit juice, whether fermented or not, and there is the additional trouble that menthol flavours persist so long. A quick rinse of water is not enough to eliminate its effects, which is presumably just what the white-coated technicians of Messrs Gibbs and Colgate work so hard to achieve. (Menthol-flavoured sweets and lozenges are best avoided by wine tasters for the same reason.)

Fortunately, I remembered that according to dental hygienists (still a fairly novel phenomenon in 1979), the brushing is much more important than the paste (though none of them is allowed to say so too loudly for fear of antagonizing the industrial giants who woo them so assiduously). From then on I stopped putting toothpaste on my toothbrush, morning or early evening, whenever I knew that the next thing I was going to taste was wine.

Experimentation with various mouthwashes demonstrated that the fierce-tasting plain Listerine mouthwash would wash away my mouth's memories of the night before without affecting wines tasted even immediately afterwards. Doubtless, however, this traditional legacy of Earl Lister's pioneer-

ing work in antiseptic surgery will soon be pushed off the shelves by the mint-flavoured version and I shall have to start my bizarre quest for the freshest of breath, cleanest of teeth and keenest of taste-buds again.

Postscript: The early morning training was probably worthwhile. It yielded Masters of Wine Rosemary George, Aileen Trew and, some years later, Jancis Robinson.

CHAPTER TWENTY-FOUR
A FOOTNOTE FROM FRANCE,
AND THE DOURO

' *"To which University," said a lady, some time since, to the late sagacious Dr Warren, "shall I send my son?" Madam," replied he, "they drink, I believe, near the same quantity of port in each of them." ' THE TIMES, 1798*

Any French gastronome would doubtless be as horrified by chapter 22 as I was when reading what Androuet, who is to *fromage* what Wisden is to cricket, wrote about Stilton: 'The incomparable Stilton is a *bleu* cheese. The English soak it for one month in sherry, or better still in port or Madeira. Then they wrap it in a white napkin and slip it into a special wooden or silver container. The Stilton, very strong and aromatic, is scooped from the top with a small spoon. It is a regal cheese, one for real connoisseurs. When you are in England, seize the chance to try a Stilton soaked in wine.'

Incroyable, n'est-ce pas? The misconceptions that are nurtured on either side of the Channel. I hardly know anyone who scoops rather than slices their Stilton, have never met anyone who admits to having poured port into one; and cannot imagine anyone dousing a decent cheese in sherry.

I prefer my port sipped in small draughts with, at most, a few nuts to soak it up. I'm not utterly convinced that port-drinking is a suitable Nordic sport. I always feel terrible after drinking vintage port in this country, but in my experience the ill-effects magically evaporate in the *quintas*, the port wine farms up the wild Douro valley in northern Portugal.

The hostess with the mostest up there, Gillyanne Robertson of Taylor's Quinta de Vargellas, makes further claims for this extraordinary corner of the world, so poor that it has been targeted as one area most in need of loans from the World Bank. After years of observation she reckons that the port and the heady Douro atmosphere combine to loosen tongues and inhibitions in a unique way. The terrace midway between the threading river below and the stars twinkling from the black up above is the secret, the social safety valve that is, for climatic reasons, missing from any home in northern Europe.

My early wine-writing years, editing the wine trade's monthly, spoilt me for vintage port. The wine trade poured it into me in liberal doses after wine trade lunches. (These seem to be on the wane, thank goodness, having been responsible for my gaining nearly two stone during that era.) For some reason — perhaps for want of a tutor in the complex art of vintage port appreciation — I remained relatively immune to its charms all those years.

It was not until a bleak January day in 1986, at a wine trade lunch in more *nouvelle vague* form, *chez* Bibendum of Primrose Hill, that my eyes were opened to the glorious potential of this sort of wine. The lunch was an intriguing and satisfying mixture. Our host, Christopher Collins, fascinatingly combines wine trading with expertise in the allied busi-

ness of perfumes. (He has also been a successful National Hunt jockey but my conversation doesn't stretch far in that direction.) The guests included not only wine luminaries, such as Patrick Grubb, recently retired from Sotheby's into business on his own account, but also the novelist and wine enthusiast, Julian Barnes. We ate sound British stuff, roast beef cold and rare, and truckle Cheddar. We drank some of the best that France had to offer: Louis Latour's Corton Charlemagne 1978, Châteaux Mouton *and* Lafite 1962 (the Mouton danced, the Lafite sang) before the *porto de luxe*.

Port-lovers will understand immediately when I explain that the port was Taylor 1948. This glowed. Extraordinarily, it combined youthful fruit and vibrancy with the sort of captivating complexity that can come only after long, slow evolution. There wasn't a trace of that rather coarse raisin note to be found in many ports. This was a wine, clearly just rounding the bend into the home straight (the racing prints were impinging on my tasting notes), rich, extremely concentrated and with great weight, yet an utterly convincing thoroughbred. Gorgeous. So *this* is what vintage port is all about.

CHAPTER TWENTY-FIVE
IN PRAISE OF ASTI SPUMANTE
SIMPLY SWEET

'Few people had intellectual pleasures sufficient to forgo the pleasures of wine. They could not otherwise contrive how to fill the interval between dinner and supper.'
DR SAMUEL JOHNSON, QUOTED IN BOSWELL'S 'LIFE'

It is odd that so many people who love champagne and Muscat de Beaumes-de-Venise are so snooty about a drink that effectively offers the pleasures of both, Asti Spumante.

Although there are lots of nasty ones about, well-made Asti Spumante is a delight: light, grapey, refreshing, flirtatious, revivifying, all of those and more. Like the literally amazingly popular *vin doux naturel* from Beaumes-de-Venise, it's made from the finest sort of Muscat grape. And though its production method owes little to Champagne, it has the great advantage (in many circumstances) of being much lower in alcohol — between 7.5 and 9 per cent. Moscato d'Asti and other Italian sparkling or fizzing (*frizzante*) Muscats can be even less potent, and sweeter. This makes them truly exceptional wines, being some of the wine world's lightest, yet also some of its sweetest, offering an unusual puzzle in matching with food.

The general rule is that a pudding wine should be at least as sweet as the pudding it accompanies. If not, the wine tastes lean and tart. If this were the only general principle applicable to finding wines for the sweet course, then Asti Spumante would be just the ticket for most sweet dishes. The trouble is, however, that its inherent lack of stuffing makes it a walkover for very rich puddings. Only something as delicate as a fairly airy syllabub or some sliced fruit does not overwhelm it. Juicy Muscat grape 'gobstoppers', perhaps made *brûlées* with a blanket of whipped cream and some fast-grilled demerara sugar, are lovely with Asti Spumante. Chocolate would be unthinkable.

Perhaps it is something to do with the Italian affinity for ice creams that makes Asti Spumante quite good with them, but any ice cream or sorbet served with wine needs to be in fairly molten state, I reckon, if it's not to anaesthetize the tasting faculties. The Italians have the right idea with the *semifreddo*, a description that seems curiously apposite for the state of so many of us Britons throughout the winter.

CHAPTER TWENTY-SIX
A SWEET TOOTH
WINE WITH PUDDINGS

'A shilling tea consisting of buttered scones or sandwiches, bread and butter, and cakes can be a paying proposition; but if jam and cream are served too, the charge must be increased to 1s. 3d.' HELEN JEROME, RUNNING A TEA-ROOM AND CATERING FOR PROFIT (1936)

It is almost impossible to grow up in farming country in the far north of England without acquiring a sweet tooth somewhere along the way.

In and around my native Kirkandrews-on-Eden (pop. 45), baking day was even more important than washing day to the local matrons in their uniform of virtuous pinnies — faded, flower-printed overalls that were wrapped tightly round an ample frame, offering whatever clothes they wore underneath (one never really found out) permanent protection from the ravages of daily life.

Baking meant the industrious, flushed but proud production of plate cakes (fruit tarts with pastry top and bottom baked on tin plates); scones pale, dark, raisin and treacle; butterfly buns (for those who had already cottoned on to the importance of presentation); squares of shortbread; Victoria

sandwich cakes; chocolate cakes glistening with their charge of butter icing; moist, dark gingerbread; and for the culinarily advanced, Swiss rolls.

Each batch was enormous. This was understandable in farmhouse kitchens, but the ovens of even the most modest bungalows would be pressed into near industrial output. And the measure of a successful tea party, or that very similar meal consumed in Cumbrian households while watching the nine o'clock news, was that after a dozen encouragements to 'Reach to' there should be *masses* left over.

For my mother and me — less so the lads, I think — the savoury part of a meal was just the necessary prelude to the really important bit, the pudding. During the summer we piled cream and sugar on to the fruits of the garden, but as soon as the mornings crispened up again, we went thankfully back to carbohydrate. And whatever the season, when I got home from school, I used to reckon it was a pretty poor tea if there were fewer than three different products of my mother's Aga on the table.

I seemed to lose my sweet tooth somewhere on the journey south, however, and like most people nowadays, have put behind me the wickedness of the day's fourth meal. I don't usually eat puddings nowadays either, but I'm certainly not one of those who are able to purse their lips and say righteously, 'Oh, I *never* eat puddings.' Though I don't expect one, and by no means always provide one, I still enjoy the sweet part of a meal, whether it offers the refreshment of a fruit-based dessert or some much less healthy pleasure.

Sweet foods make difficult partners for many wines, however. Dry wines are hopeless. They taste thin and mean with anything sweet (which is why most wine enthusiasts have been trained to forswear redcurrant jelly with their lamb, though have been getting mightily flustered by the many *nouvelle* encroachments of fruits on to the dinner plate). I just can't understand why so many otherwise civilized people continue to drink their (inevitably dry and usually red) main course wine with something sweet. Water would be so much more sensible, not just because it isn't spoilt by sweet food, but because it comes at a stage in a meal when a bit of respite from the demon drink would usually be no bad thing.

The obvious wines to serve with sweet foods are, of course, sweet themselves. But as outlined in the previous chapter, the wine needs to be pretty sweet to stand up to really sweet food. Fine Auslesen from Germany are absolutely gorgeous on their own, before or after a meal, but can be clobbered by anything sweeter than a few slices of fruit. This is why Muscat de Beaumes-de-Venise has been such a hit; it's so sweet it can stand up to almost any pudding. Sauternes is generally a good bet too because of its high alcohol content, 13 degrees and more, but the quality varies enormously. I find that a really good Sauternes is almost more delicious with something salty, such as Roquefort or another blue cheese. There is such a complex mesh of flavours in a fine, mature Sauternes that most puddings are themselves fighting it for attention, instead of providing a straightforward and complete contrast.

The one sweet substance that everyone agrees is difficult to marry with wine is chocolate because of its tongue-coating texture. As I discovered when researching an entire article on this absorbing subject, only very alcoholic, very sweet, but non-tannic wines will do. In my experience, the only two candidates are dark and raisiny: Australian Liqueur Muscat from north-east Victoria, and Malaga from criminal golfer country in the deep south of Spain. The firm with the almost Esperanto name of Scholtz Hermanos is the leading light of Malaga the wine, though its blend of this gloriously old-fashioned wine has been getting rather drier and almost, perish the thought, modern. Liqueur Muscats, bless them, come in many more styles and sizes, but each shares the alcohol (over 18 per cent), the complexity (from usually well over eight years in cask), and the teeth-rotting sweetness that give this unique style of wine the guts to stand up to even a liqueur chocolate (to which, despite the name, the wines bear no relation).

I've found Liqueur Muscats to be extremely useful wines with all manner of sweet things, in fact, ranging from the exotic flavour and texture of a mango, through chocolate mousse and cheese to the homely comfort of a creamy rice pudding (given vital spark in this household by a few shavings of lemon peel).

The only precise combination of sweet wine and sweet food I've found absolutely perfect, in that the wine picks up notes from the food and the wine's residual sugar is at exactly the right level of sweetness for my particular recipe, is *tarte Tatin* with the unique botrytized white burgundy from Thévenet-Wicart, their Mâcon-Villages Clessé 1983 Cuvée Spéciale Botrytis. Young Chardonnay often has a distinct appley note, and in this wine (of which I must admit I was extremely wary when I first heard about it, having never experienced successful sweet Chardonnay), it combines with a wonderful purity, refreshing acidity and lots and lots of the buttery, caster sugar sweetness that is so important in making the caramel part of this delicious upside-down apple tart. (The tart, supposedly invented by the Tatin sisters, is much better with Cox's orange pippins than with any French apple I've come across, and a waste of time with anything as woody and relatively flabby as the average pear.)

We keep having to re-order the extraordinary Mâcon, and soon, no doubt, the world will run out of it — until Burgundy is again given a vintage of such exceptional ripeness.

CHAPTER TWENTY-SEVEN

SUNDAY LUNCH IN TUSCANY

VIN SANTO & BISCOTTI

'The man who could sit under the shade of his own vine with his wife and children about him, and the ripe clusters hanging within their reach, and not feel the highest enjoyment is incapable of happiness and does not know what the word means.' JAMES BUSBY, FATHER OF AUSTRALIAN VITICULTURE

I remember so clearly the first time I experienced the delights of sanctioned dunking. It was in a small restaurant in the Tuscan countryside where some friends kindly took me for Sunday lunch, a welcome respite from staff meals at the luxury hotel which employed me that summer nearly twenty years ago.

I'd never seen anything like this public acknowledgment, nay, celebration, of the fact, ignored in most British restaurants, that most adults were, at one stage in their lives, children. The place was full of large family parties, *nonno* and at least one *nonna* at the end of each long table, with several sets of parents around the edges, interspersed with progeny of all ages, from only a few weeks old through, most audibly, two- to ten-year-olds.

When there was food on their plates the children attacked it with gusto. When there was none they raced about, in and out of the restaurant, paying visits to other tables, and happily ruining the ultra-chic, multi-lira outfits into which they had so carefully been stuffed that morning. The air was riven with squeals and shrieks. The bead curtain played its own percussion as it swung under constant pressure from tiny but fast-moving bodies. The management was entranced, and so were the customers, including this one.

I remember nothing of what we ate and drank, except the very end of the meal when we were served a magical yellow-amber liquid in funny little conical glasses and charmless little dry biscuits spiked with aniseed and almonds. They could, and obviously should, be magically transformed into meltingly soft mouthfuls of molten Tuscany by a few seconds' immersion in this, the true amber nectar: *vin santo*, or 'holy wine'.

Like an aromatic cross between sherry and a Chaume sweet Loire wine, proper *vin santo* is made by fermenting

87

mainly Malvasia grapes that have been part-dried to raisin status by hanging them in sweet-smelling, dusty chambers. It has a lustrous tang about it that makes a gorgeous end to a meal, with or without the dunking ritual.

Top quality *vin santo* is still a relative rarity outside Tuscany (and quite difficult to find even in that sanctified hill country itself), but the biscuits are easily bought in the Italian delicatessens of Soho. My London variant on the Tuscan experience, oft-practised at the end of a simple supper, is to immerse *cantucci* in an inch or two of good quality Amontillado or Oloroso sherry (so much cheaper than *vin santo* too). It works well with almost-dry sherries, and works up a keen thirst for my puny but favourite end to a meal — a nice cup of tea.

SOME USEFUL UK ADDRESSES

GOOD ALL-ROUND WINE MERCHANTS:

Adnams, The Crown, High Street, Southwold, Suffolk

H Allen Smith, 14/25 Scala Street, London W1 and WC1, NW3 and SW3

Bibendum, 113 Regent's Park Road, London NW1

D Byrne, 12 King Street, Clitheroe, Lancashire

Corney & Barrow, 12 Helmet Row, London EC1, various branches in the City and at 190 Kensington Park Road, W11

Eldridge Pope, Weymouth Avenue, Dorchester, plus 'Wine Libraries' in Fleet Street, EC4 and Exeter

Grape Ideas, 3-5 Hythe Bridge Street, Oxford

Peter Green, 37 A/B Warrender Park Road, Edinburgh

Haynes Hanson & Clark, 17 Lettice Street London SW6 and 36 Kensington Church Street, London W8

The Hungerford Wine Company, 128 High Street, Hungerford, Berkshire

Lay & Wheeler, 6 Culver Street and Gosbecks Road Wine Market, Colchester, Essex

Tanners, 26 Wyle Cop, Shrewsbury, Shropshire and branches

La Vigneronne, 105 Old Brompton Road, London SW7

MAINLY MAIL ORDER:

Berkmann Wine Cellars, 12 Brewery Road, London N7

Richard Harvey Wines, The Auction House, East Street, Wimborne Minster, Dorset

Hicks & Don, 4 The Market Place, Westbury, Wiltshire

O W Loeb, 64 Southwark Bridge Road, London SE1

Morris & Verdin, 28 Churton Street, London SW1

Reid Wines, Hallatrow, near Bristol (and a wine warehouse outside Sevenoaks)

Philip Tite Fine Wines, 73 Whitehall Park Road, London W4

Henry Townsend, York House, Oxford Road, Beaconsfield, Hertfordshire

Windrush Wines, Cecily Hill Barracks, Cirencester, Gloucestershire

The Wine Society, Gunnels Wood Road, Stevenage, Hertfordshire

CHAINS WHICH TRY HARDER:

Davisons, Majestic, Oddbins, Sainsbury's, Tesco, Waitrose

SPECIFIC WINES MENTIONED IN CHAPTERS:

CHAPTER 3. Ridge Zinfandels are usually stocked by Adnams of Southwold, Les Amis du Vin, 51 Chiltern Street, London W1 and The Winery, 2 Clifton Road, London W9

The taramasalata is available only at the Rosslyn Delicatessen, 56 Rosslyn Hill, London NW3

CHAPTER 5. Madeira specialists are Ellis Son & Vidler, Cliffe Cellars, 12/13 Cliffe Estate, Lewes, East Sussex and 57 Cambridge Street, London SW1.

Those who take more than usual trouble with sherry include Berry Bros & Rudd, 3 St James's Street, London SW1; Tanners, 26 Wyle Cop, Shrewsbury; and Hicks & Don, 4 The Market Place, Westbury, Wiltshire.

CHAPTERS 7 and 25. Merchants with particularly good selections of Italian wines include The Market and Le Provencal shops around London; Winecellars Warehouse, 153/155

Wandsworth High Street, London SW18; Millevini, 3 Middlewood Road, High Lane, Stockport, Cheshire; Adnams of Southwold; Oddbins; Ostler's, 63a Clerkenwell Road, London EC1.

CHAPTER 8. An excellent range of Beaujolais, including the wines of Ernest Aujas, is available from Roger Harris, Loke Farm, Weston Longville, Norwich. Berkmann Wine Cellars of 12 Brewery Road, London N7 specialise in the famous Beaujolais of Georges Duboeuf.

CHAPTER 11. Most of the merchants listed above take trouble with their burgundy, of both colours. Particularly good for white burgundy are Lay & Wheeler, Corney & Barrow, Adnams, Henry Townsend, Haynes Hanson & Clark, Berkmann Wine Cellars, Morris & Verdin of 28 Churton Street, London SW1 and Domaine Direct, 29 Wilmington Square, London WC1.

CHAPTER 13. Yapp Bros of Mere, Wiltshire have some very good Bandol.

CHAPTERS 15 and 19. Alsace wines are a speciality of L'Alsacien, 105 Old Brompton Road, London SW7

CHAPTER 17. Tyrrell's wines are imported by Christopher & Co, 7a Grafton Street, London W1. Australian specialists are Ostlers and Alex Findlater, 77 Abbey Road, London NW8; Ostlers, also have some good New Zealand wines, and the specialist importer is Fine Wines of New Zealand, P O Box 476, London NW5.

CHAPTER 26. The Australian specialists are best for Australian Liqueur Muscats while importers of Scholtz Malaga are Laymont & Shaw, The Old Chapel, Mill Pool, Truro, Cornwall.

The Mâcon-Villages Clessé 1983 Cuvée Speciale Botrytis has been stocked by Adnams of Southwold, Les Amis du Vin, Justerini & Brooks of 61 St James's Street, London SW1 and 39 George Street, Edinburgh and Windrush Wines of Cecily Hill Barracks, Cirencester, Gloucestershire.

CHAPTER 27. Vin Santo is probably best obtained from one of the Italian specialists, but Sainsbury's introduced a fairly commercial one to their shelves in Spring 1987.

INDEX

ACKNOWLEDGEMENTS

For permission to reproduce the following extracts at chapter headings the publisher gratefully acknowledges the following:

Chapter 3 – Auberon Waugh – WAUGH ON WINE – Fourth Estate Ltd (Publishers)

Chapter 8 – Maurice Healy – STAY ME WITH FLAGONS – Alexander M Sullivan

Chapter 9 – *Gourmandise at Yquem* is reprinted by kind permission of *A La Carte*

Chapter 10 – Waverly Root – THE FOOD OF FRANCE – Reprinted by permission of Alfred A Knopf Inc. Copyright © 1958, 1966 by Waverly Root

Chapter 18 – *The Economist* August 2nd 1980

Chapter 19 – John Masefield – CAPTAIN STRATTON'S FANCY – The Society of Authors

Chapter 26 – Helen Jerome – RUNNING A TEA-ROOM AND CATERING FOR PROFIT – Pitman Publishing, London